In My Opinion ...

A Photocopiable Collection of Opinion Gap Discussion Topics

Second Edition

Phil Keegan

PR LINGUA
LEARNING

Pro Lingua Learning
PO Box 4467
Rockville, MD 20849 USA
Office: 301-424-8900
Orders: 800-888-4741
Email: info@ProLinguaLearning.com
Web: www.ProLinguaLearning.com

*At Pro Lingua Learning
our objective is to foster an approach
to learning and teaching that we call
interplay, the **inter**action of language
learners and teachers with their materials,
with the language and culture,
and with each other in active, creative,
and productive **play.***

This book was designed and set by Arthur A. Burrows using two text types, Arno Pro and Bradley Hand. The cover design is by A.A. Burrows using photos © by Jafaris Mustafa and Bruno Passigatti. In the book, the icon of the cards is © Eric Wong, and that of the questionnaire is © Feng Yu. All are from the Dreamstime.com Agency.

Second edition 2019.

Acknowledgements

I have been teaching for quite a long time, more than twenty years now, and many people – writers, teachers, and, of course, students – have influenced me. I don't know how to thank and acknowledge all of them, and I apologize for any omissions in the following.

As for writers, Michael Lewis and Steven Krashen have been massive influences. Many thanks indeed to them. Although not specifically EFL books, *Freedom to Learn* by Carl Rogers and *A Different Kind of Teacher* by Tony Humphreys are marvelous works which I would highly recommend to anyone involved in teaching.

I first got turned on to using questionnaires for teaching by Gillian Porter Ladouse's excellent book, *Speaking Personally*.

As for teachers, my colleagues and friends Brian Robinson and Sean McLaughlin were very supportive and helpful when I was a rookie in Stuttgart, Germany, in 1985. Between 1989 and 1993, I continued my professional development in Adana, Turkey, at Gülek Özel Lisesi, and greatly enjoyed my time there. Many thanks to Yasa Çeliktaş and Atilla Gazioğlu.

However, I developed hugely as a teacher during the two years I spent at what was then International House Hastings between 1994 and 1996. It was there that I did my RSA Diploma under the excellent tutelage of Jim Scrivener and Allan Brammall, and where I also had the pleasure of working with a truly inspiring group of colleagues. With great affection and gratitude I would like to thank the aforementioned Jim and Allan as well as Jude Wilkinson, Ellie Spicer-Lundholm, Claire Rickards, Bill Harris, Colin Spicer, Vic Richardson, Bruce McGowen, Adrian Underhill, Rosie McAndrew, Deb Barratt, and others whose names have regrettably deserted me in the intervening years.

This book was written during the many years I spent in Austria, and many friends and colleagues there lent considerable help and support. I would particularly like to thank Hans Reitbauer from The Technical University in Graz, as well as Ross Little, Anita Töcterle and Rebecca Llewellyn (who gave me the idea for Unit 45). I would like to thank Emma Somerville for eagle-eyed proof reading and many thanks also to Josef Schneeberger. I am also very grateful indeed to the many students in Austria who were the unwitting guinea pigs for these activities and who gave me very helpful feedback on them. Danke schön!

Phil Keegan 2009

Phil has revised his book and added new topics for this 2019 edition.

Contents

Introduction

This book consists of activities to get learners of English speaking. That's it really.

Each activity allows learners the opportunity to speak and express their opinions on a wide range of issues. Preceding the activities, there are two pages of Useful Phrases for the learners. These are only a few of the possible phrases, and you should feel free to add your own.

The book is based on the principles of communicative language teaching and, to a large extent, the principles of the natural approach. First and foremost is the idea that learners need speaking practice and need time and space to be able to express themselves in the new language if they are to make progress.

I often tell my learners that learning a new language is like playing a musical instrument. Let's take the piano as an example; you can listen to piano music, you can read books about the piano and books of music theory, and all this will help you understand the piano and piano music. However, if you don't actually put your fingers on the keyboard and try to do it, if you don't actually *play* the piano, you will not be able to play it. You can only really learn to play by doing it.

Furthermore, even when you can play, you still need to practice regularly to keep and improve your proficiency.

User Friendly 📖 Cards and 📄 Questionnaires

Most of these activities are very simple to prepare and execute. Some activities require you to make **cards** from a master (but once made they can be reused again and again, especially if you laminate them), and the other activities consist of putting your learners into pairs or groups and handing out a **questionnaire**. If you feel it is necessary, you can pre-teach some vocabulary; with this in mind, potentially difficult words are provided in the teacher's notes. **Lesson-by-lesson teacher's notes start on page 67 at the back of the book.**

Throughout the notes there are many suggestions for songs to introduce the activity. Using music to set the stage can help participants be more relaxed when they are challenged to express and explain their opinions.

These activities work with learners from intermediate to advanced proficiency level.

The Teacher's Role

I have assumed throughout that these activities will be used with a class, and have indicated that the learners should be put into small groups of three to six. If the activity is a card game, you just need a set of cards for each group. If it is a questionnaire, give out a questionnaire to each student or to each group.

However, these activities can also be used by pairs, or even in a one-to-one, tutorial situation, in which you work with a single learner and give your opinions.

When working with groups, your role is to circulate, giving help and support as necessary. There are great opportunities for vocabulary input when these activities are going on.

However, and this is important, I would strongly advise against correcting any grammar mistakes during the activities. Let your learners try to express themselves. Interrupting their discussions with corrections can be very counter-productive. I have taught many learners who are afraid of making mistakes. Usually, because they are so used to being constantly corrected, it is difficult to make them talk. To be blunt, if students are afraid to talk, they quite simply never will learn. To return to the musical instrument analogy: people make a lot of mistakes when they are learning to play an instrument, but no one should get upset about those mistakes. It is all part of the learning process. Learners should be allowed to learn from their mistakes without feeling bad about them. Mistakes are friends. They show the learners where they need to go next.

Furthermore, it is a rare person indeed who is perfect in a second language, so why should your learners be perfect? During these activities, it is much better if you just make a note of any mistakes and deal with them at a later time, without even pointing out who made the mistake. These are free-speaking activities, so allow your learners to be free! Give them time and space to express themselves, and don't pester them with corrections while they are trying to do so.

This book is not meant to be worked through like a textbook. This is a stand-alone, photocopyable resource book to be turned to whenever you feel your learners need some speaking practice. Most activities work well on their own, but many can also be either warm-ups or follow-ups for listenings or readings that you are working with. It is also not always necessary to do the whole activity. With some activities it is possible to do some of the questions and return to the activity at a later time.

Not all activities work with all groups. I have included a "things to look out for" section in the teacher's notes with some guidelines to help on this point.

That's all, really. Have fun observing and listening to your learners speak!

Phil Keegan

Useful Phrases

The following phrases can be used to ask for opinions:

- What's your opinion of...?
- What's your position on...?
- I'd like to hear your views on...
- What do you think?/What do you think about...?
- What about you, John, What's your opinion?/ What's your opinion on this?

The following phrases can be used to give opinions:

- In my opinion,
- I think...
- If you ask me,
- It seems to me that...
- As I see it,

The following phrases can be used to agree with someone:

- I agree.
- You're right.
- I think we agree with each other on this point.
- That's true.
- Good point!/That's a good point.

The following phrases can be used to agree strongly with someone:

- I completely agree.
- You're absolutely right.
- Oh, absolutely!

The following phrases can be used to agree partly with someone:

- I agree up to a point, but...
- I agree with you on the whole, but it could be argued that...
- I see your point, but...
- I hear what you're saying, but...

The following phrases can be used to disagree with someone:

- I don't completely agree with you on that.
- I really can't accept your point of view/what you are saying.
- I feel I must disagree.
- I disagree.

The following phrases can be used to disagree strongly with someone:

- I disagree entirely.
- I don't agree at all.
- You're completely mistaken.
- What you are saying is just not possible.

If you don't know someone well or if you are in a formal situation, it is important to be tactful and diplomatic when you disagree with someone. The following phrases can be used to warn people that you are going to disagree with them, which has the effect of making your disagreement softer and more polite:

- I'm afraid...(e.g. I'm afraid I have to disagree with you on that point.)
- I'm sorry... (e.g. I'm sorry but I don't agree.)
- With respect...(e.g. With respect, I think you've got your facts wrong.)
- Would you mind if I... (e.g. Would you mind if I ask a question?)
- You have a point of course, but…
- Sorry, but I'm not sure...

If you want or need to interrupt a discussion to give your opinion, you can say:

- I'm sorry to interrupt, but could I just say…
- Pardon my interruption, but...
- Forgive me for interrupting, but...
- May I, please, say that I think that...
- Could I just say something?
- Could I just jump in here?
- May I ask a question about that?

Teenage students should have much more influence on how schools are run.

1

Euthanasia should be legal.

1

Killing animals is murder and should not be allowed for any reason.

1

The main problem with western society is that most people are not religious and do not go to church.

1

Teachers should be paid much more money.

1

Smoking should be banned in all public buildings, including restaurants and bars.

1

It is not possible for a woman to be the leader of a country; it's a man's job.

1

Homosexuals should have the same rights as heterosexuals, including the right to marry, adopt children, and so on.

1

Teachers should be paid according to how good they are, not according to how long they have been teaching.

1

Professional athletes make too much money.

1

People should spend more time learning the languages of their neighboring countries and less time learning English.

1

The United States is too powerful.

1

Western society is too materialistic.

1

University education should be open and free to everybody.

1

All young men and women should do at least one year of compulsory military service.

1

All immigration should be stopped immediately.

1

Health care should be provided by private companies.

1

Soft drugs such as marijuana should be legalized.

1

Young people have too much freedom nowadays.

1

People should pay if they want to drive their cars into cities.

1

Unemployed people should do some kind of community service in return for unemployment benefits.

1

Private citizens should not own guns.

1

The Internet is dangerous.

1

The invasion of Iraq was wrong.

1

2 ● I think...

With your partner(s) discuss your answers to the questions below.
For a shorter and easier discussion, do only the first 12.

1. What is your idea of perfect happiness?

2. What is your biggest fear?

3. Which living person do you most admire?

4. What do you dislike most about yourself?

5. What are you most proud of?

6. In which situations do you lie?

7. What is your favorite smell?

8. How do you relax?

9. When and where were you happiest?

10. What makes you most depressed?

11. Which talent would you most like to have?

12. What is your biggest regret?

13. Who is (or was) the greatest love of your life?

14. What is the greatest love of your life?

15. Which living person do you most despise?

16. What objects do you always carry with you?

17. How would you like to die?

18. Which single thing, except for more money, would improve the quality of your life?

19. What is your biggest extravagance?

20. What do you think of this questionnaire?

3 ● What do you think?

Ask your partner(s) about

Family

3

Ask your partner(s) about

Holidays

3

Ask your partner(s) about

Their hometown

3

Ask your partner(s) about

Books

3

Ask your partner(s) about

Work

3

Ask your partner(s) about

Free time

3

Ask your partner(s) about

Love

3

Ask your partner(s) about

Famous People

3

Ask your partner(s) about

Pets

3

Ask your partner(s) about

Politics

3

Ask your partner(s) about

Religion

3

Ask your partner(s) about

Ambitions

3

Ask your partner(s) about

Children

3

Ask your partner(s) about

Hopes for the future

3

Ask your partner(s) about

Films

3

Ask your partner(s) about

Art

3

Ask your partner(s) about

Food

3

Ask your partner(s) about

The environment

3

Ask your partner(s) about

Traveling

3

Ask your partner(s) about

Cars

3

Ask your partner(s) about

Health

3

Ask your partner(s) about

Reading

3

Ask your partner(s) about

Plans for next year

3

Ask your partner(s) about

Clothes

3

First go through this questionnaire on your own. Then work with a partner or in a small group. For each 'yes' you have checked, tell your partner(s) the story of what happened.

1. Have you ever broken a bone in your body?
   ☐ *yes*　　☐ *no*

2. Have you ever been late for something really important?
   ☐ *yes*　　☐ *no*

3. Have you ever broken a valuable object?
   ☐ *yes*　　☐ *no*

4. Have you ever broken a law?
   ☐ *yes*　　☐ *no*

5. Have you ever failed an exam that you expected to pass?
   ☐ *yes*　　☐ *no*

6. Have you ever had an automobile accident?
   ☐ *yes*　　☐ *no*

7. Have you ever fallen asleep at work?
   ☐ *yes*　　☐ *no*

8. Have you ever fallen down stairs?
   ☐ *yes*　　☐ *no*

9. Have you ever lost your temper?
   ☐ *yes*　　☐ *no*

10. Have you ever fallen in love at first sight?
    ☐ *yes*　　☐ *no*

11. Have you ever broken someone's heart?
    ☐ *yes*　　☐ *no*

12. Have you ever written a love poem?
    ☐ *yes*　　☐ *no*

13. Have you ever cycled more than 60 miles in one day?
    ☐ *yes*　　☐ *no*

14. Have you ever lost your keys?
    ☐ *yes*　　☐ *no*

15. Have you ever met anyone famous?
    ☐ *yes*　　☐ *no*

16. Have you ever had a bad vacation?
    ☐ *yes*　　☐ *no*

17. Have you ever wanted to be the opposite sex?
    ☐ *yes*　　☐ *no*

18. Have you ever wished you were someone else?
    ☐ *yes*　　☐ *no*

5 ● Annoying Habits

Which habits do you dislike in other people?

> **You can use the following phrases to express yourself:**
>
> - I dislike it when people … …
> - It's (really/extremely/incredibly/so) annoying when people …
> - It really upsets me when people … …
> - I can't stand it when people … …
> - It really gets on my nerves when people … …
> - It's extremely irritating when people … …
> - It really gets my goat when people … …

Grade the following habits from 0 = Not annoying at all, to 5 = Extremely annoying.
Explain your answers to your partner(s).

1. ____ Making noises when eating
2. ____ Talking when watching a film or TV
3. ____ Talking to cats
4. ____ Blowing one's nose in public
5. ____ Saying the same thing again
6. ____ Kissing in public
7. ____ Not paying attention to what people are saying
8. ____ Smoking cigarettes
9. ____ Not saying "please" or "thank you"
10. ____ Laughing or talking very loudly
11. ____ Talking loudly on a cell phone
12. ____ Saying things like "I'm on the plane now" on a cell phone
13. ____ Not switching off a cell phone in the movies/theater/classroom
14. ____ Not looking into people's eyes when greeting them
15. ____ Showing off
16. ____ Eating snacks during meetings/lessons
17. ____ Not covering one's mouth when yawning
18. ____ Not returning phone calls
19. ____ Complaining about the weather
20. ____ Playing loud music
21. ____ Arriving late
22. ____ Interrupting
23. ____ Talking too much
24. ____ Chewing gum

Do you have any of the above habits?
What other habits annoy you?

6 ● Are you a communicator?

First answer these questions about yourself. Then discuss them with your partner(s).

1. I write emails or letters to friends and/or relatives.
   ☐ often ☐ sometimes ☐ rarely ☐ never

2. I meet friends socially at least twice a week.
   ☐ often ☐ sometimes ☐ rarely ☐ never

3. If I am angry with someone I tell them about it clearly and calmly.
   ☐ often ☐ sometimes ☐ rarely ☐ never

4. I enjoy paying compliments to friends and/or colleagues.
   ☐ often ☐ sometimes ☐ rarely ☐ never

5. I love going to parties.
   ☐ often ☐ sometimes ☐ rarely ☐ never

6. If I thought my boss was doing something wrong, I would tell them about it.
   ☐ often ☐ sometimes ☐ rarely ☐ never

7. I feel comfortable in a crowd.
   ☐ often ☐ sometimes ☐ rarely ☐ never

8. I talk about my problems to one or two close friends.
   ☐ often ☐ sometimes ☐ rarely ☐ never

9. People come to me for advice.
   ☐ often ☐ sometimes ☐ rarely ☐ never

10. I prefer group sports to solo sports.
    ☐ often ☐ sometimes ☐ rarely ☐ never

11. I would rather play cards or Trivial Pursuit with friends than play a computer game on my own.
    ☐ often ☐ sometimes ☐ rarely ☐ never

12. I enjoy teaching other people what I know how to do.
    ☐ often ☐ sometimes ☐ rarely ☐ never

7 ● Computers

Interview your partner(s) and find out exactly what they do with computers.
Fill in the following table with their answers.
Finally, discuss the questions on the next page.

Activity	Yes or No?	How Often?	Details
Writing			
Working with photos			
Studying			
Working			
Taking courses			
Skyping/Facetime			
Researching			
Shopping			
Emailing			
Instant messaging			
Blogging			
Visiting chat rooms			
Facebook/Instagram			
Telephoning			
Playing games			
Paying bills/banking			
Listening to music			
Watching videos			
Using Internet Cafes			
Other			

First, answer the following questions. Then discuss them with your partner(s):

1. How many hours a day on average do you spend in front of a computer?
   - During the week: ☐ 0-3 ☐ 3-6 ☐ 6-9 ☐ 9-12 ☐ more than 12
   - On the weekend: ☐ 0-3 ☐ 3-6 ☐ 6-9 ☐ 9-12 ☐ more than 12

2. Of the above time, how much is your free time and how much is for your studies or work?

3. Of the above time, how much was useful or enjoyable and how much was basically a waste of time?

4. What's the best thing about computers for you?

5. Have you had any bad experiences with computers?

6. Can you imagine life without computers?

7. Do you, or does anyone you know, have a problem with computer/internet addiction?
   If yes, give details. (Be honest!)

8 ● How green are you?

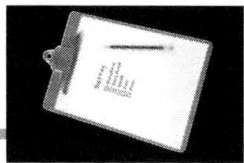

Answer the following questions, checking the boxes as appropriate. Then discuss your answers. Finally, check your score to see how green you are.

1. What is your main means of transport to get to your place of work or study?
- ☐ Walking
- ☐ Cycling
- ☐ Public transportation
- ☐ Car (alone)
- ☐ Car (shared)

2. Which of the following do you regularly recycle?
- ☐ Paper
- ☐ Plastic
- ☐ Glass
- ☐ Metal
- ☐ Compost

3. When you do your household shopping, how do you usually bring your goods home?
- ☐ Get or buy plastic bags from the store each time
- ☐ Reuse plastic bags from the store
- ☐ Use other reusable bags or a shopping trolley

4. When you do your food shopping, do you usually buy:
- ☐ Fresh food
- ☐ Frozen food

5. Which of the following appliances do you usually leave on standby overnight?
- ☐ TV
- ☐ Stereo
- ☐ Computers
- ☐ Coffee machines

6. What kind of light bulbs do you use in your house?
- ☐ Low-energy compact fluorescent
- ☐ Standard

7. How many of the following are used to supply energy for your home?
- ☐ Solar energy
- ☐ Wind power
- ☐ Other renewable energy source

8. When you go out on weekends or in the evenings, which form of transportation do you usually use?
- ☐ Walking
- ☐ Cycling
- ☐ Public transportation
- ☐ Car (alone)
- ☐ Car (shared)

Key for Activity 8, How Green Are You?

Question 1

      A and B: plus three points

      C: plus 2 points

      D: minus 3 points

      E: 0 points   My points _____

Question 2

      Plus 2 points for each one checked   My points _____

Question 3

      A: minus 3 points

      B: plus 1 point

      C: plus 3 points   My points _____

Question 4

      A: plus 3 points

      B: minus 2 points   My points _____

Question 5

      Minus 2 points for each one checked   My points _____

Question 6

      A: plus 3 points

      B: minus 2 points   My points _____

Question 7

      Plus 5 points for each one checked   My points _____

Question 8

      A and B: plus three points

      C: plus 2 points

      D: minus 3 points

      E: 0 points   My points _____

                                        My total _____

The more points you have, the less damage you are doing to the environment!

9 • Clothes

How interested are you in clothes? 9	Do you like to go clothes shopping alone or with friends? 9
Do you think clothes are important? 9	Do you have a favorite designer or label? 9
Do you have clothes that you wear only on special occasions? 9	Where do you usually buy clothes? 9
Does your country of origin have a traditional or national costume? Please describe it. Do you own such a costume? 9	How would you describe your personal clothes style or dress sense? 9
How often do you buy new clothes? 9	Are you more or less interested in clothes now than when you were younger? 9
How much money do you spend on clothes per year? 9	Why do you think teenagers are often so interested in clothes? 9

Do children in your country of origin wear a school uniform? What's your opinion of school uniforms?

9

How many pairs of shoes do you own?

9

Do you think you judge other people on their dress sense?

9

Do you know where the clothes you buy are made?

9

Why is it important in business to look smart?

9

Are you interested in fashion shows? Have you ever been to one?

9

What do you think of professional models? Are they good role models for young people?

9

How much do you usually spend getting your hair done?

9

What do you think about the fashion industry?

9

What is the most expensive item of clothes you have ever bought?

9

Would you like to be a clothes designer?

9

Does buying new clothes make you happy?

9

10 ● Shoes

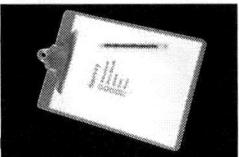

With your partner(s) discuss your answers to the questions below.

1. How many pairs of shoes do you own? (Approximately)

2. How many of these shoes do you wear regularly?

3. Do you have any pairs that you have only worn once?

4. What are your three favorite pairs of shoes?

5. If you had to pick one pair only, which pair would you pick?

6. What is the most expensive pair of shoes you own?

7. Which pair or pairs have you had the longest?

8. Are you planning to buy more shoes soon?

9. How often do you buy shoes?

10. Are there any shoes you want to buy but which are too expensive?

11. Are shoes important to you?

12. When you meet other people, do you notice their shoes?

13. Do shoes say something about a person's character/personality?

11 ● Dreams

Work with a partner or with a small group. Answer the following questions.
Explain in detail the reasons for your answers.

1. What is your dream job?

2. Can you describe your dream house?

3. Where is your dream place to live? (Which town/city/country?)

4. What is your dream car?

5. What is your
   • dream height?
   • dream weight?

6. Who is your dream man/woman? (You can choose anyone in the world, alive or dead.)

7. If you are interested in a team sport, such as soccer, make a dream team of your favorite players. (You can choose any players in the world.)

12 • Getting the News

How often do you read, watch, or listen to the news? How do you get your news?
Complete the table below and then discuss it with your partner(s).

✔		Details	How Often?
	TV		
	Radio		
	Newspaper		
	Magazines		
	Internet		
	• Websites		
	• Blogs		
	• Chat rooms		
	• Other		
	Talking to . . .		
	• Friends		
	• Family members		
	• Colleagues		
	• Teachers		
	• Other		

13 ● Animals, Meat, Vegetarianism

How do you feel about animals in general?

13

How often do you eat meat?

13

Tell your partner(s) about the pets you have had and how you felt about them.

13

If you eat meat, where do you buy it, and where does it come from?

13

If you have never had any pets, why?

13

What do you think about animal rights and animal rights protestors?

13

Do pet owners ever annoy you?

13

What's your opinion about wearing fur or leather?

13

Do you have any opinions on vegetarians and vegetarianism?

13

What do you think about hunting as a pastime or hobby?

13

Are there many vegetarians in your country of origin?

13

What do you think about using animals for medical research?

13

14 ● Emotions

In English there is the expression 'to keep a stiff upper lip.' It means that you should not show your emotions in public. According to some people, the British think this is important. Japanese people also have the reputation for not showing their emotions, whereas Mediterranean people such as the Spanish and the Italians have the reputation of being very open with their emotions. People often say that women are much more emotional than men. Are these stereotypes true?

How emotional are you? Complete the following questionnaire, and then discuss your answers with your partner(s).

1. You should never cry in public.
   ☐ agree   ☐ disagree   ☐ it depends

2. I find it embarrassing when people kiss passionately in public.
   ☐ agree   ☐ disagree   ☐ it depends

3. I don't like to listen to other people's problems.
   ☐ agree   ☐ disagree   ☐ it depends

4. You should never argue with your girl/boyfriend or spouse in front of other people.
   ☐ agree   ☐ disagree   ☐ it depends

5. I don't like my friends to touch me/put their arms around me when I am upset.
   ☐ agree   ☐ disagree   ☐ it depends

6. When you are having a good time in a pub or restaurant, you should still be careful not to disturb other people.
   ☐ agree   ☐ disagree   ☐ it depends

7. When I get angry I usually keep it inside me.
   ☐ agree   ☐ disagree   ☐ it depends

8. I find it difficult to talk about personal problems.
   ☐ agree   ☐ disagree   ☐ it depends

9. I find it ridiculous that people can get so emotional about such things as football.
   ☐ agree   ☐ disagree   ☐ it depends

10. When John Lennon was killed and when Princess Diana died, people who had never even met them were openly crying in the street; I cannot understand this.
    ☐ agree   ☐ disagree   ☐ it depends

11. If I am attracted to someone, I find it quite hard to show it.
    ☐ agree   ☐ disagree   ☐ it depends

12. I never cry when watching sad/sentimental films.
    ☐ agree   ☐ disagree   ☐ it depends

15 ● Friendship

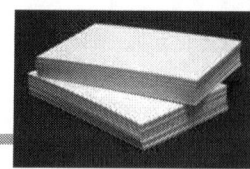

What are the qualities you value in friends?

15

Do you think there are differences between male-male friendships and female-female friendships?

15

In your free time, do you prefer to be with friends or with your family?

15

Think of the close friend you have known longest. How long have you known them? How did you become close? Has your friendship changed much over time?

15

How many really close friends do you have? Would you like to have more ?

15

Can you think of a time when you felt let down by a friend? What happened? Did you ever talk about how you felt? If yes, how did they react? If no, would you like to talk to this friend?

15

Do you make friends easily or do you need a long time to be close to someone?

15

When you were at school did you have one special friend or were you in a group, or did you prefer to be alone?

15

How often do you meet up with your closest friends? What sort of things do you do together?

15

What do you think this quote means? Do you agree?
   "Whoever says friendship is easy has obviously never had a true friend!"

15

Do you have more male or more female friends? What's your opinion of friendships between men and women?

15

What do you think this quote means? Do you agree?
   "True friendship is like sound health; the value of it is seldom known until it is lost."

15

16 ● Gays and Lesbians

Do you understand these words?

gay   lesbian   LGBT   homosexual   homosexuality
homophobic   homophobia   sexual orientation
bisexual   transgender   gender neutral
straight   heterosexual   pansexual

Answer these questions with your partner(s). Give reasons for your answers.

1. Should gays and lesbians be allowed to:

    Marry?
    ☐ yes   ☐ no ☐ it depends

    Adopt children?
    ☐ yes   ☐ no ☐ it depends

    Serve in the military?
    ☐ yes   ☐ no ☐ it depends

    Work in schools as supervisors/teachers?
    ☐ yes   ☐ no ☐ it depends

    Work as religious leaders?
    ☐ yes   ☐ no ☐ it depends

    Kiss/be affectionate in public places?
    ☐ yes   ☐ no ☐ it depends

2. Do you think gays and lesbians should "come out" (tell people that they are gay/lesbian) or should they keep quiet about their sexuality?

3. Do you think homosexuality is genetic, or is it the result of upbringing?

Answer these questions with a partner or in a small group. Give reasons for your answers.

1. How would you feel and what would you do in the following situations?

   A colleague at work/a classmate at school with whom you have to work closely tells you he is gay.

   You find out that your nine-year old son's male teacher is gay.

   Your younger sister tells you she is a lesbian.

   Your hairdresser tells you he is gay.

   Your boyfriend/girlfriend tells you that he/she is bisexual.

   You are the manager of a company and you are looking for someone to be your assistant. The best candidate for the job is a woman who is openly gay.

2. Are gays and lesbians generally accepted in your country of origin?

3. Are there many well-known people who are openly gay?

4. Are there any openly gay politicians in your country of origin?

5. What would happen in your country of origin if your leader (prime minister, president, or some other national leader) suddenly came out and said, "I am gay"?

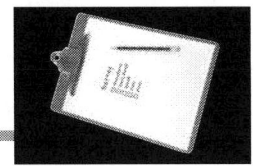

Answer and discuss the following questions with your partner(s).

1. If a husband and wife both work full-time, they should share the housework equally and fairly.
    ☐ Agree   ☐ Disagree   ☐ It depends

2. Many husbands think they do half of the housework, but in reality women do more.
    ☐ Agree   ☐ Disagree   ☐ It depends

3. If a woman wants a successful career, she has to work harder and better than her male colleagues.
    ☐ Agree   ☐ Disagree   ☐ It depends

4. The husband should have the last word on big decisions.
    ☐ Agree   ☐ Disagree   ☐ It depends

5. Men are better at managing money than women.
    ☐ Agree   ☐ Disagree   ☐ It depends

6. If a couple decide to have children, the woman should stay at home to look after them.
    ☐ Agree   ☐ Disagree   ☐ It depends

7. Women are more organized and more efficient than men.
    ☐ Agree   ☐ Disagree   ☐ It depends

8. Women's emotional reactions cause a lot of problems in relationships.
    ☐ Agree   ☐ Disagree   ☐ It depends

9. Women are more intuitive than men.
    ☐ Agree   ☐ Disagree   ☐ It depends

10. Many men can't accept a female boss.
    ☐ Agree   ☐ Disagree   ☐ It depends

11. Men often find it difficult to talk about their feelings and emotions.
    ☐ Agree   ☐ Disagree   ☐ It depends

12. There is too much pressure on women to look thin and beautiful.
    ☐ Agree   ☐ Disagree   ☐ It depends

13. It is not realistic to expect a relationship to last a lifetime.
    ☐ Agree   ☐ Disagree   ☐ It depends

14. Women are better drivers than men.
    ☐ Agree   ☐ Disagree   ☐ It depends

18 • Family

1. How important is your family to you?

2. Generally speaking, in your culture, is family very important?

3. How many members are there in your immediate family?

4. How many members are there, approximately, in your extended family?

5. Write the names of four members from your immediate and extended family and then talk to your partners about these relatives.

6. How often do you see members of your immediate and extended family?

7. When you meet family member that you don't live with, what do you do together?

8. Is there anyone in your family that you are especially close to?

9. Is there anyone in your family that you don't like?

10. Is there a head of the family in your family?

Are there are a lot of different dialects in your country of origin?

19

Which foreign languages do people learn in your country of origin?

19

Do different people from your country of origin ever have problems understanding each other?

19

Which foreign languages, other than English, do you know, and how well can you speak them?

19

In your mother tongue, do you speak a dialect? If yes, do you always speak it or only in special situations?

19

How do you feel about learning English?

19

In your country of origin, is it generally acceptable to speak a dialect? Are some dialects more acceptable than others?

19

Do you think it is important to have a world language? Is English the best choice?

19

Are there big differences between dialects in your country of origin and the standard language? If yes, give some examples.

19

Native English speakers often do not learn another language. How do you feel about that?

19

Are your country of origin's dialects based on geographical/regional factors only, or are other factors also relevant?

19

Which foreign languages, other than English, would you like to be able to speak?

19

20 ● Life Choices

Put the following things in order of importance to you, where 1 = the most important and 5 = the least important:

- Job/career or studies
- Hobbies/free time activities
- Close relationship (husband/wife/boyfriend/girlfriend)
- Family
- Friends

1. _____
2. _____
3. _____
4. _____
5. _____

Compare with your partner(s).

*

Now, put the above categories in order according to how much time you need for them (or choose to spend on them) in a normal week, where 1 = the most time, and 5 = the least time.

1. _____
2. _____
3. _____
4. _____
5. _____

Compare with your partner(s) again.

Are you happy with this situation or is there anything you would like to change? For example, do you work too much? Do you have too little time for hobbies or friends or family? Do you spend too much time watching TV?

Discuss with your partner(s).

21 ● Work

Make a list below of things you like about your job and things you don't really like, then compare and discuss with your partner(s).

☺ Like ☺	☹ Don't like ☹

Which of these words describe your feelings about your work? Choose as many as you want, and you can also add your own words.

challenging   frustrating   rewarding   tedious   interesting
exciting   repetitive   fun   satisfying

If you didn't need the money, would you work? Why/Why not?

In Britain, more than 65% of winners of the lottery jackpot say that winning the lottery made them unhappy in the end. What could be the reasons for this? Discuss with your partner(s).

22 ● Vacations

Answer the following questions and discuss your answers with partners.

When you go on vacation, do you usually:

	Always	*Often*	*Sometimes*	*Rarely*	*Seldom*
Stay in a hotel or bed and breakfast?					
Arrange a homestay?					
Arrange accommodation through a crowd-sourcing site such as *Airbnb* or *Couchsurfing*?					
Stay with friends?					
Stay with family?					
Go camping?					
Sleep outdoors:					
Other?					

Which of the following holidays have you already tried?

	Yes✓	*When & Where?*
Beach resort holiday		
Holiday in the mountains		
Walking holiday		
Cycling holiday		
Adventure holiday		
Visiting a city		
Staying somewhere quiet in the countryside		
Holiday on a boat		
Holiday in a nightclub area		
A camping holiday		
A train journey		
Visiting friends/family in another city or country		
A vacation for religious or spiritual reasons		
A vacation to experience and learn about another culture		
A vacation to learn something, for example painting or pottery or a foreign language		

Talk to your partners about each vacation you have already tried. Was it fun? Talk about the good experiences you had. Talk about any bad experiences.

Are there any kinds of vacation that you have not yet tried that you would like to try?

What would be your nightmare vacation?

Who do you normally go on vacation with?

Generally, do you prefer to take vacations in your own country or to go abroad or both?

Try to imagine your dream vacation and talk to your partners about it.

23 ● How Do You Relax?

After a day of work or study (or both work and study), which of the following ways of relaxing do you like to do? Complete the table on your own then compare with some partners and talk about how you relax.

Activity	Alone	With Others	How Often?
Watching TV			
Watching Movies			
Doing Sports			
Doing yoga			
Watching Sports			
Going to bar/pub for a drink			
Having a drink at home			
Going out to eat			
Cooking at home			
Playing with your children			
Drinking tea or coffee			
Chatting to someone			
Going online			
Reading a book			
Listening to music			
Playing a musical instrument			
Reading a newspaper			
Going for a walk			
Playing with pets/walking a dog			
Playing computer games			
Going to a museum/art gallery			
Doing something artistic/creative			
Spending time outdoors/in nature			
Taking a bath			
Sleeping			
Being alone			
Meditating			
Getting a massage			
Eating something sweet			
Writing a diary/journal			
Dancing			

Do you have any ways of relaxing which are not on this list? Talk to your partners about them if you do.

24 ● Insurance

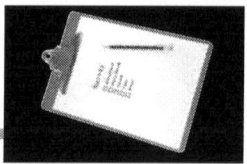

Which of the following types of insurance do you have? Fill in the table and then compare with some partners and discuss.

	Yes	No
Car (or other vehicle) insurance		
Home insurance		
Fire insurance		
Health insurance		
Dental insurance		
Life insurance		
Travel insurance		
Pet insurance		
Musical instrument insurance		
A pension plan		
Mobile phone insurance		
Accident insurance		
Camera insurance		
Laptop insurance		
Bicycle insurance		
Liability insurance		
Income protection insurance		
Funeral insurance		
Flood insurance		
Earthquake insurance		
Income protection insurance		
Other type of insurance		

Discuss these questions with a partner:

How much do you spend per year on insurance? *Do you consider that reasonable?*

How often do you make claims on your insurance?

What was the last insurance claim you made? Why did you make it? *How did the company respond?*

Has an insurance company ever refused to pay out after a claim?

How important is insurance?

Should affordable health care be a universal right?

25 • Military Service

Answer and discuss the following questions with your partner(s).

1. It is every citizen's duty to defend their homeland.

   ☐ agree strongly ☐ agree ☐ not sure/it depends ☐ disagree ☐ disagree strongly

2. Compulsory military service is the best way of ensuring that there are people who are able to defend their homeland.

   ☐ agree strongly ☐ agree ☐ not sure/it depends ☐ disagree ☐ disagree strongly

3. If a country has compulsory military service, both men and women should do it.

   ☐ agree strongly ☐ agree ☐ not sure/it depends ☐ disagree ☐ disagree strongly

4. Everyone should have the right to be a conscientious objector to compulsory military service.

   ☐ agree strongly ☐ agree ☐ not sure/it depends ☐ disagree ☐ disagree strongly

5. Compulsory military service is no longer necessary.

   ☐ agree strongly ☐ agree ☐ not sure/it depends ☐ disagree ☐ disagree strongly

6. Compulsory military service serves no purpose. Having a well-trained, professional army is the only way to protect a country.

   ☐ agree strongly ☐ agree ☐ not sure/it depends ☐ disagree ☐ disagree strongly

7. Compulsory military service is forced slavery to the state and is therefore a violation of human rights.

   ☐ agree strongly ☐ agree ☐ not sure/it depends ☐ disagree ☐ disagree strongly

8. Politicians would be less keen to go to war if they knew that their own sons and daughters could be drafted.

   ☐ agree strongly ☐ agree ☐ not sure/it depends ☐ disagree ☐ disagree strongly

9. A period of compulsory military service can be an important learning experience for young people.

   ☐ agree strongly ☐ agree ☐ not sure/it depends ☐ disagree ☐ disagree strongly

10. It's good for a country if everyone has the experience of being in the military.

    ☐ agree strongly ☐ agree ☐ not sure/it depends ☐ disagree ☐ disagree strongly

11. Generally speaking, are you:

    ☐ in favor of compulsory military service?
    ☐ against compulsory military service?

26 ● Money

Complete the following alone, and then discuss your answers with your partner(s).

1. Money is very important to me.
   □ very true □ true □ it depends □ not really true □ completely untrue

2. I usually know how much money I've got on me.
   □ very true □ true □ it depends □ not really true □ completely untrue

3. I usually know how much money I've got in the bank.
   □ very true □ true □ it depends □ not really true □ completely untrue

4. Not having enough money has sometimes made me very unhappy.
   □ very true □ true □ it depends □ not really true □ completely untrue

5. I enjoy talking about money.
   □ very true □ true □ it depends □ not really true □ completely untrue

6. Having more money would make a big difference to my life.
   □ very true □ true □ it depends □ not really true □ completely untrue

7. The behavior of rich people sometimes makes me angry.
   □ very true □ true □ it depends □ not really true □ completely untrue

8. When I think of the poverty in the third world, I sometimes feel guilty.
   □ very true □ true □ it depends □ not really true □ completely untrue

9. I hate being in debt.
   □ very true □ true □ it depends □ not really true □ completely untrue

10. Credit cards are an invitation to spend money that you don't have.
    □ very true □ true □ it depends □ not really true □ completely untrue

11. As I get older, money is becoming more important to me.
    □ very true □ true □ it depends □ not really true □ completely untrue

12. I really like spending money.
    □ very true □ true □ it depends □ not really true □ completely untrue

13. I find it quite hard to save money.
    □ very true □ true □ it depends □ not really true □ completely untrue

14. I go to a lot of trouble to buy things at the lowest price I can find.
    □ very true □ true □ it depends □ not really true □ completely untrue

15. Money is freedom.
    □ very true □ true □ it depends □ not really true □ completely untrue

16. I like reading the financial pages of the newspaper.
    □ very true □ true □ it depends □ not really true □ completely untrue

17. There are some things that I really hate spending money on.
    □ very true □ true □ it depends □ not really true □ completely untrue

18. It is sometimes fun to gamble.
    □ very true □ true □ it depends □ not really true □ completely untrue

19. I dislike lending and borrowing money.
    □ very true □ true □ it depends □ not really true □ completely untrue

20. I hate banks.
    □ very true □ true □ it depends □ not really true □ completely untrue

27 ● Music

What was the first recording that you bought with your own money? Do you still listen to it sometimes?

27

What are your five all-time favorite pieces of music?

27

In which form do you get your music these days (radio, MP3 downloads, streaming on wireless (smart) speakers using digital music services like Google Play Music or Spotify, etc.)?

27

When do you listen to music?

27

How often do you buy MP3s or CD's?

27

Why do you listen to music?

27

What kind or kinds of music do you listen to nowadays?

27

How often do you listen to live music?

27

Have your tastes in music changed from when you were younger? If yes, how and why?

27

Are your tastes in music different from your parents'?

27

Do you have a favorite singer/group/musician/composer?

27

What was the best concert you have ever been to?

27

Have you ever been to a bad concert?

27

Can you sing?

27

Does music ever get on your nerves?

27

Did your parents sing to you when you were a child? Can you remember the songs?

27

Why do you think teenagers are often so fascinated by music?

27

How do you feel about your country of origin's folk/traditional music?

27

Can you play, or have you ever played, any instruments?

27

Do you sing in the bath/shower?

27

Is there an instrument you would really like to be able to play?

27

Who is the biggest pop star in your country of origin? Describe them.

27

Can you read music?

27

Who is the greatest composer of all time?

27

28 ● Names

Write a name in each box as indicated and then work with your partner(s) and talk about the people you have named.

1. The most important person in your life at the moment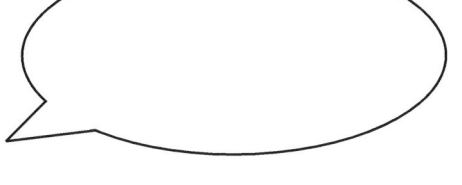

2. Someone who influenced you in the past

3. Someone you don't like

4. Someone you know personally and admire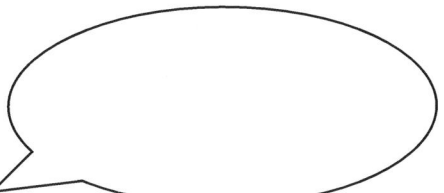

5. A famous person you would like to meet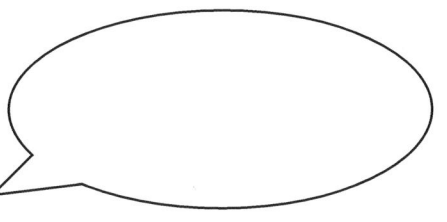

6. Anyone you would like to talk about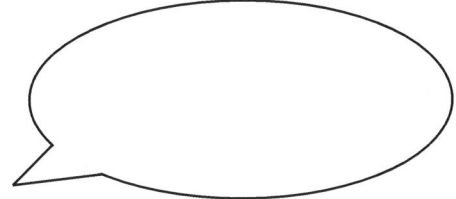

29 ● Patriotism

Tell your partners about your country of origin.

29

What is your opinion of patriotism?

29

Tell your partners where your parents came from.

29

What do you think about stereotypes other nationalities have about your region or country?

29

What is your citizenship status now? How do you feel about that?

29

Can you name some well-known people from your country of origin? Do you feel in any way connected to them or proud of them? Why/Why not?

29

Do you feel the same way about your country of origin as your parents do/did?

29

If you had the power to change your country of origin, what would you change and why?

29

What country is more important to you in terms of your personal identity?

29

Have you ever been embarrassed to be from your country of origin? If yes, explain.

29

Do you know the words to your country of origin's national anthem? Can you translate them or summarize them in English?

29

Where in the world would you most like to live? Explain the reasons for your choice.

29

Who is the head of state of your country of origin? What do you think of them? 30	What do you think of your country of origin's politicians? Are they good or bad? Honest or dishonest? 30
Does your head of state have political power or are they just a figurehead? Is your head of state popular with the people? 30	Can you remember any political scandals in your country of origin? 30
Talk about your political system: • Who is allowed to vote? • How is the government elected? • How is the leader of the government elected? 30	Are there many female politicians in your country of origin? What about people from ethnic minorities? 30
What do you think of your country of origin's political system? 30	What do you think of American politicians? 30
What are the main political parties in your country of origin? Which party is in power? 30	What do you think about the political situation of the country you are now living in? 30
What do you think of your country of origin's political parties? 30	Which country do you think has the best political system? Why? 30

Think back to your childhood.
Which special rituals or traditions do
you remember?

31

Do you think traditions are always good,
or should some traditions die out?

31

Is there any special religious/cultural
meaning to the rituals or traditions of
your country of origin?

31

Do you think your country of origin is
losing its traditions, or are they still
very important?

31

Did your family have its own special
rituals?

31

Are any modern rituals developing in your
country of origin?

31

When you meet up with your family
these days, do you still practice any
old family rituals?

31

Which traditions from your country of
origin do you really like?

31

What rituals or traditions are still
important to you?

31

What are your favorite memories from
childhood?

31

Do you or will you teach any traditions to
your children?

31

Do you think of yourself as a traditional or
a very modern person?

31

32 • The Death Penalty

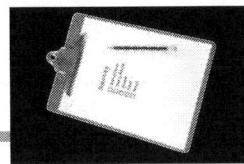

Do you agree or disagree with the following statements? Fill in the questionnaire.
Then discuss with your partner(s).

1. The death penalty is a deterrent; that is, when there is a death penalty, there are fewer serious crimes.

    ☐ agree strongly   ☐ agree   ☐ it depends   ☐ disagree   ☐ disagree strongly

2. It is cheaper to have the death penalty than to keep someone in prison for a lifetime.

    ☐ agree strongly   ☐ agree   ☐ it depends   ☐ disagree   ☐ disagree strongly

3. Some crimes are so bad that the criminals deserve to die.

    ☐ agree strongly   ☐ agree   ☐ it depends   ☐ disagree   ☐ disagree strongly

4. The death penalty is a cruel and inhuman punishment.

    ☐ agree strongly   ☐ agree   ☐ it depends   ☐ disagree   ☐ disagree strongly

5. When a country has the death penalty, it tells its people that killing someone is a solution to a problem. This creates a culture of violence.

    ☐ agree strongly   ☐ agree   ☐ it depends   ☐ disagree   ☐ disagree strongly

6. The death penalty is not safe; the risk of an innocent person dying is too high.

    ☐ agree strongly   ☐ agree   ☐ it depends   ☐ disagree   ☐ disagree strongly

7. The death penalty is never used fairly; certain groups of people are always treated worse than others.

    ☐ agree strongly   ☐ agree   ☐ it depends   ☐ disagree   ☐ disagree strongly

8. It is not fair to the families of a murder victim that the killer can live a nice life in prison, getting three meals a day and having the chance one day to be free again.

    ☐ agree strongly   ☐ agree   ☐ it depends   ☐ disagree   ☐ disagree strongly

9. The death penalty is the only real justice for a brutal murderer.

    ☐ agree strongly   ☐ agree   ☐ it depends   ☐ disagree   ☐ disagree strongly

10. The death penalty is immoral.

    ☐ agree strongly   ☐ agree   ☐ it depends   ☐ disagree   ☐ disagree strongly

What is/are the main religion/religions in your country of origin?

33

In some countries religion is taught at school, but in other countries it is forbidden in schools. What's the situation in your country of origin, and what's your opinion on this?

33

How important is religion in your country of origin?

33

Are there any conflicts in your country of origin because of religion?

33

How many people in your country of origin really practice their religion according to its rules and how many people just pay lip service to religion?

33

Do you think there are conflicts around the world because of religion?

33

Is it important in your country of origin that politicians appear to be religious? For example, would it be possible for the president or leader of your country of origin to be an atheist?

33

What do you know about religious conflicts in the past?

33

Are minority religions and/or atheism accepted in your country of origin?

33

How important is religion to you personally? What does it mean to you? Do you have a sense of God?

33

Do you think an atheist could ever be President of the USA?

33

In your opinion, what place should religion have in the modern world?

33

34 ● Ethics

Answer the following questions <u>honestly</u>, then work in small groups and discuss your answers. You must work on the principle that <u>you will never get into trouble in any way</u>, whatever answer you choose.

1. A builder does some work on your house and you are very satisfied. It should cost about $2500, but he says that if you pay him in cash and he doesn't give you an invoice, you can pay 25% less (the work will still be covered by guarantee). Would you:

    a. Refuse the offer and ask for a proper invoice?
    b. Accept the offer and pay him in cash?
    c. Try to negotiate a bigger reduction for paying cash?

2. You run your own company and have recently been negotiating a possible contract with the government of a Third World country. The contract would be worth about $15,000,000. The minister you have been dealing with has made it clear that if you give him a 'sweetener' of $500,000 in cash, under the table, he will give the contract to you. Would you:

    a. Stop all negotiations with this government?
    b. Agree to give him the money?
    c. Agree to give him the money and ask him if he wants anything else in
       case there are more contracts in the future)?

3. You are having problems in a really difficult and important exam. Would you:

    a. Just try to do your best?
    b. Cheat?
    c. Pretend to have a heart attack?

4. You invite your friends to an expensive restaurant. After an excellent meal with good service you get the bill and notice that they have forgotten to charge you for your desserts. Would you:

    a. Tell the server about the mistake and pay for the desserts?
    b. Say nothing and pay the bill?
    c. Ask your friends what to do?

5. You drop your expensive camera from your balcony at home and it smashes. Your insurance does not cover such accidents. However, if you tell the insurance company that your camera was stolen while you were on holiday, they will pay for a new one. Would you do this?

    a. No
    b. Yes
    c. Yes, and also claim for an expensive designer camera bag that you never owned

6. You oversleep one morning and miss a very important meeting at work. You have never done this before. Would you:

    a. Apologise to your boss and tell them that you overslept?
    b. Make an excuse such as your car broke down or the train was late because there was a dead cow on the
       tracks (or some other fake excuse?).
    c. Call your boss and tell him/her that a family member has died (or some
       other lie) and that you need more time off work?

7. Your mother has a new hairstyle that she's very proud of but you think she looks ridiculous. Would you:

    a. Tell her what you really think?
    b. Say nothing?
    c. Tell her she looks fine?

8. The tax office makes a mistake and repays you $3000. You know 100% for sure that this is a mistake. Would you:

    a. Tell them they made a mistake and arrange to pay the money back?
    b. Do nothing?
    c. Contribute the money to charity.

35 • School

The cards on this page are for people who have left school.

What type of secondary/high school did you go to? Was there a special focus (e.g. science or languages, etc.)? Was it co-educational? 35	Which teachers, both good and bad, do you remember? 35
Did you like school? Why/Why not? 35	Was bullying ever a problem at your school? 35
Were you a good student? 35	What do you think about the school system today in your country of origin? Is it really good or do you think it could be better? 35
Were you ever in trouble at a school? 35	What do you think about teachers in your country of origin? 35
Which subject or subjects did you like best? Why did you like this subject/these subjects? 35	Do teachers in your country of origin earn a good salary? 35
Which subjects didn't you like? Why didn't you like them? 35	Do teachers have too many days off? 35

The cards on this page are for people who are attending school.

Do you like school? Why/why not? 35	Is bullying ever a problem at your school? 35
Are you a good student? 35	In your opinion, what are the qualities of a good teacher? 35
Have you ever been in trouble at school? 35	Do teachers have too many days off? 35
Which subjects do you like best? Why do you like these subjects? 35	What do you think about the school system today in your country of origin? Is it really good or do you think it could be better? 35
Which subjects don't you like? Why don't you like them? 35	What do you think about teachers in your country of origin? 35
What do you think about homework? Too much? Is it worthwhile? 35	Do teachers in your country of origin earn a good salary? 35

36 ● Smoking

Compare your answers to these questions with those of your partner(s).

1. If you are a smoker, or have ever smoked, tell your partner(s) about your first cigarette: Why did you smoke it? How old were you? How did you feel, physically and mentally?

2. If you have never smoked, tell your partner(s) why.

3. If you are a smoker, answer the following questions with your partner(s):

   • In which situations do you usually smoke?

   • Why do you smoke when there is so much evidence about the unhealthy effects of smoking?

   • Have you ever tried to give up? If yes, what happened?

4. If you are a non-smoker:

   • Why do you think people smoke?

   • Has anyone ever put pressure on you to smoke?

   • Does smoking ever bother you? If yes, in which situations?

   • Does it bother you if your boyfriend/husband or girlfriend/wife smokes?

Smoking should be banned in all public places, including restaurants and bars.

36

Banning smoking is only the beginning of the government's wish to control all aspects of our lives.

36

It is every individual's right to smoke if they want.

36

If people smoke in public they damage other people's health too. That shouldn't be allowed.

36

If you don't want to breathe cigarette smoke, you shouldn't go to bars.

36

All governments need the income from taxes on cigarettes.

36

People who smoke take more breaks at work and therefore work less than non-smokers: That is not fair.

36

People who smoke should pay more for their health insurance.

36

The government should increase the tax on cigarettes in order to encourage people to give up smoking.

36

Tobacco companies should pay people compensation for the damage to their health caused by smoking.

36

High tax on cigarettes is unfair for poor people.

36

Smoking is cool.

36

37 • Drinking

According to the British government, men should drink no more than 21 units of alcohol per week and women no more than 14 (An alcohol unit is a glass of wine or beer).

What do you think of these recommendations?

Why do people drink alcohol? Check the boxes which are relevant to you.

✔

	I never drink alcohol.
	I drink alcohol when I go out with friends.
	I drink alcohol to help me relax and deal with stress.
	I drink alcohol when I want to celebrate something.
	I drink alcohol because other people want me to.
	I drink alcohol when I am bored.
	I drink alcohol because I like the taste.
	I drink alcohol because everyone I know drinks it.
	I drink alcohol because it is cool.
	I drink alcohol because I like to get drunk.
	I drink alcohol because I am shy/ because it gives me courage to do things.
	I drink alcohol because it makes life more interesting.
	I don't really know why I drink alcohol; I just do.
	I drink alcohol because I am addicted to it.
	I drink alcohol when I eat something good.
	Other reasons for drinking alcohol

Work with a partner or in a small group. Compare your answers and discuss; for example, if you drink alcohol to celebrate something, why do you drink alcohol and not something else? If you never drink alcohol, is there a special reason for this? If you like to get drunk, why do you like to get drunk? Discuss with your partner(s).

Soft drugs should be legalized. 38	Drugs help people escape from their boring, everyday lives. 38
All drugs should be legalized. 38	The laws regulating drugs should be even stricter than they are now. 38
If all drugs were legalized, the government could control their use much more effectively and would also be able to make money by taxing drugs. 38	Many great artists/writers/musicians could not have been so creative without drugs. 38
Soft drugs are less dangerous than alcohol. 38	People who take drugs are weak. 38
Soft drugs are gateway drugs; that is, they open the door to harder drugs. 38	Legalizing drugs would reduce crime. 38
Experimenting with drugs is a part of growing up. 38	Governments spend millions of dollars every year trying to stop people from taking drugs but people still take them. It is a waste of money. 38

What are the biggest sports in your country of origin? 39	How do you feel about the top athletes from your country of origin? 39
How do you feel about sports? 39	What do you think about the money that modern professional athletes earn? 39
Do you do any sports? If yes, which ones and how often do you do them, and why? If no, why not? 39	Most professional baseball players have higher salaries than the president of the US. What do you think about that? 39
Are there any sports you haven't done which you would like to try? 39	Some people think that international sports competitions bring nations together and help keep the peace. What's your opinion? 39
Which sports do you enjoy as a spectator? 39	What do you think about the use of drugs in sports? 39
Do you have a favorite athlete or a favorite team? 39	Which sports do you do, or did you do when you were younger? 39

How often do you think about time?

40

How much time do you spend doing things you don't want to do:

- at work?
- in your free time?

40

How much of your free time do you really enjoy?

40

How often do you say 'I don't have time,' and how often is it really true?

40

How much time per week do you waste on doing nothing at all?

40

If the day had four extra hours, what would you do with them?

40

Did you waste a lot of time in the past? Do you have any regrets?

40

Are you good at managing your time?

40

How much time per day is just for you and for nobody or nothing else?

40

What is boredom for you?

40

When you are at work, how much time do you spend actually working?

40

What does time mean for you?

40

41 ● Technology

How do you feel about technology in general?

41

How well do you understand the technology you use?

41

How much has technology changed during your lifetime?

41

Are you able to repair any of your mechanical or electronic devices when there are problems?

41

Have all the technological changes in your lifetime been for the better, or are there some disadvantages?

41

Do you ever get frustrated or angry with technology?

41

Of the mechanical or electronic devices you own or use, which are the most useful?

41

Do you see any dangers with technology?

41

If you had to live with just one mechanical or electronic device, which one would you choose?

41

Do you like science fiction films or books?

41

What is the most worthless mechanical or electronic device you have ever heard of?

41

How will technology change the future?

41

42 ● Smart Phones

1. What do you use your phone for? Fill in the table then compare with a partner.

Activity	✓ Yes	How Often?
Making phone calls		
Messaging		
Surfing the internet		
Online banking		
Online shopping		
Playing games		
Listening to music		
Studying/learning something new		
Reading maps		
Taking photos/videos		
Editing photos/videos		
Checking the weather		
Using as a torch/flashlight		
Using as a calculator		
Doing puzzles/brain exercises		
Checking traffic		
Buying tickets for events (such as cinema or sports events)		
Looking for flights/train tickets/bus tickets		
Checking in for a flight		
Checking timetables		
Watching videos		
Monitoring your heart rate		
Tuning a musical instrument		
Checking the stock market		
Managing a blog		
Reading a book/magazine		
As a mirror		

2. What kind of smart phone (or phones) do you own?

3. How long have you had the one you have now? Are you planning to buy another one?

4. How many smart phones have you previously owned?

5. How much did your phone cost? Do you think it was good value for money?

6. How often do you check your phone during the day?

7. Which Apps do you use most and why?

8. Are there any other uses for your smart phone that are not on this list?

9. What, for you, is the best thing about your smart phone?

43 • Social Media

Which social media sites are you registered with?

What is/are your favorite site(s)? Why do you like them?

What do you use social media sites for? Tick each box that is true for you and then discuss with your partner(s).

Activity	Yes✓	How often?
To know what friends are doing		
To stay in contact with family		
To pass the time		
To find interesting or funny content		
To get news about current events		
To share my opinions		
To share photos or videos		
To meet new people		
To share details of my everyday life		
To network with other people		
For my job		
To look for new jobs		
For studying		
To promote myself		
Other reasons (give details)		

What device do you use to visit social media sites?

Tick each box that is true for you and then discuss with your partner(s).
- o   Desktop computer
- o   Laptop
- o   Smart phone
- o   Tablet

How many hours a day do you spend on social media sites?
☐ less than one ☐ 1-2 ☐ 2-4 ☒☐ 4-6 ☐ More than six

Do you or does anyone you know spend too much time on social media sites?

Do you worry about privacy or about the amount of information that some social media sites collect about you?

What are the dangers of using social media sites?

44 ● Socializing

How often do you do the following things? Complete the table and then discuss with your partners.

	With Friends	How often?	With Family	How often?	Alone	How often?
Go to the movies						
Go to a coffee shop						
Go to restaurants						
Go to a bar/pub						
Go to eat ice cream						
Go to see live theatre						
Go to sports events						
Go to listen to live music						
Go to a park/nature reserve						
Go to a zoo						
Go to a museum						
Go to botanical gardens						
Go to an art exhibition or arts festival						
Go to a gaming center						
Go shopping with friends						
Do sports with friends						
Go on a weekend break						
Visit a historical site						
Attend a religious ceremony/ritual						
Other social event						

45 ● Transportation

How do you get to your place of work or study?
Check each box that is relevant.

✔		**Why?**
	on foot	
	by car	
	by bicycle	
	by train	
	by subway	
	by bus	
	by trolley/tram	
	by cab/taxi	
	by motorcycle/moped	
	by boat/ferry	
	other	

Compare with a partner or in a small group. Tell your partner(s) why you use the mode or modes of transportation you use. Are there any alternatives to the mode(s) you use?

Discuss these questions with your partner(s):

- How do most people in your country of origin get to their place or work or study?

- Is public transportation relatively cheap or expensive in your country of origin?
  What do you think of the public transportation system in your country of origin –
  is it good or bad, efficient or inefficient?

- Do many people in your country of origin own a car, or do most people use public transportation?

- If public transportation were cheaper and/or more efficient, would more people use it?

- How expensive is gasoline or diesel fuel in your country of origin?

- Many governments are trying very hard to make people use their cars less and public transportation more. What do you think about that? What's the situation in your country of origin?

46 ● Reading

Which of the following things have you read in the past week? Fill in the table and give some details; then discuss and compare with your partner(s).

✔ | | **Details**

✔		Details
	Novels	
	Graphic novels	
	Non-fiction	
	Instruction/Technical manuals	
	Religious books or texts	
	Websites	
	Newpapers	
	Magazines	
	Comic books or strips	
	Advertising slogans	
	Recipes	
	Signs	
	Other people's t-shirts	
	Timetables	

	Bulletin boards	
	White/Blackboards	
	Restaurant menus	
	Bumper stickers	
	Emails	
	Catalogues	
	Faxes	
	Reports	
	Dictionaries	
	Letters	
	Blogs	
	Other	

Discuss these questions with your partner(s).

How often do you read books just for pleasure?

How important is reading for pleasure for you?

What do you do more: watch TV or read books? Explain your answer.

Do you think children read enough nowadays?

47 ● Television

Look at the types of TV programs below. Which programs do you watch?
Check the boxes and give some details; then compare with your partner(s).

✔		**Details**
	sitcoms	
	soaps	
	documentaries	
	religious programs	
	music programs	
	talk shows	
	political debates	
	children's programs	
	cooking programs	
	history programs	
	quiz shows	
	the news	
	detective/police series	
	wildlife programs	
	drama series	
	comedy shows	
	sports programs	
	travel programs	
	reality shows	
	the weather	
	other	

TV Guessing Game

Here are some comments some people made about TV programs.
What type of program do you think they are talking about?
Write your answers, and then compare answers with your partner(s).

> **(You can use the language of speculation:**
> *That could be……..* or, if you are really sure, *That must be………)*

- They make it look so easy and everything they make is so perfect. In my kitchen it never works like that.

- It is pointless. They just say their own opinion and never listen to what the other person has to say. It is a waste of time.

- They are just eating each other or having sex. It's horrible.

- When I watch it I just get depressed.

- It is so predictable. They always get the bad guy in the end.

- I dislike the fake laughter in the background.

- I love hearing about distant places that I will probably never be able to visit myself.

- It is great to relax and have a good laugh.

- I just like to switch off my brain.

What are your favorite programs?	Of the hours you spend in front of the TV, how much do you really enjoy and how much is just passing time or a waste of time?
47	47
Which programs don't you like?	Do you ever fall asleep in front of the TV?
47	47
How much TV do you watch on average (per day or per week)?	Do you watch too much TV?
47	47
Why do you watch TV?	Do you think children today watch too much TV? If yes, what can be done about it?
47	47
Does watching TV make you happy?	Is there too much sex and violence on TV?
47	47
Does watching TV ever make you angry?	Overall, do you think TV is a good thing or a bad thing?
47	47

48 ● Movies

Do you have a favorite movie or type of movie? 48	What do you think of Hollywood movies? 48
Do you have a favorite movie star? 48	Modern blockbuster movies can cost hundreds of millions of dollars to make. What do you think about that? 48
Do you prefer to watch movies at a theater or at home? 48	Does your country of origin have a movie industry? 48
To watch a movie on your TV, computer, cellphone, do you use a subscription to a steaming service, pay to watch the specific film, or buy a DVD? What do you do? 48	Talk about the worst movies you have seen. 48
How often do you go to a movie theater? How expensive are they in your country of origin? 48	Are movies just entertainment for you, or do you think they have an important part to play in our society? 48
Do you usually read the reviews of movies before you watch them? Why/Why not? 48	Who are more famous in your country of origin: American movie stars or your own country's movie stars? 48

49 ● Food

What have you eaten so far today? Fill in the table.

	Breakfast	Lunch	Evening Meal	Snacks
Today				

What did you eat yesterday and the day before? Fill in the table.

	Breakfast	Lunch	Evening Meal	Snacks
Yesterday				
The Day Before Yesterday				

1. Are these tables a good example of your typical eating habits?

2. Compare with your partner(s):

   - Who ate the healthiest food?
   - Who ate the most food?
   - Are you normally a big eater?
   - Generally, do you try to follow a healthy diet?

3. Can you cook?
   - If no, why not?
   - If yes, how did you learn, and what can you cook?

What was your favorite food when you were a child? Do you still like to eat it? What's your favorite food now?

49

How popular is fast food in your country of origin?

49

Is there any food you really don't like?

49

How important is it for you to eat regularly with your family or friends?

49

What's your favorite time of the day to eat?

49

How often do you eat in restaurants?

49

Is your diet very different from what you ate as a child?

49

What is your country of origin's national dish or dishes? Do you miss your country of origin's cuisine?

49

What is the strangest thing you have ever eaten?

49

Are you getting hungry?

49

What's your opinion of fast food and the big fast food companies?

49

Is there an expression or phrase that you say in your language before eating? What do you think about the fact that there is no such standard phrase in English?

49

50 ● Popular Beverages

Which of the following do you drink? Interview your partner(s) and find out what they drink.

✔	Drink	Details	How often?	Why?
	Tap water			
	Bottled water			
	Soft drinks (colas, etc.)			
	Milk			
	Tea			
	Coffee			
	Fruit juice			
	Energy drinks			
	Soda water			
	Hot chocolate			
	Vegetable juice			
	Alcohol-free beer			
	Other non-alcoholic beverages			
	Other			

How do you feel about health care and health insurance in this country?

51

What do you think of modern Western medicine? Are too many vaccines used?

51

What is the situation in your country of origin regarding health care and insurance?

51

What kinds of alternative medicine do you know about?

51

Is free and good health care a basic human right?

51

Have you tried any kinds of alternative medicine?

51

What do you think of the standard of health care in your country of origin? Is it the same for everyone, or does it depend on money?

51

How often do you take pain killers or other non-prescription drugs?

51

What do you think of the doctors in your country of origin? Are they good?

51

What do you think about taking health care supplements such as vitamin pills?

51

Do doctors in your country of origin earn a lot of money? What about nurses and other health care professionals?

51

Do you really take care of your health?

- What do you do that's really healthy?
- What do you do that's really not healthy?

51

What time do you usually get up during the week? 52	At which part of your working day are you most productive? 52
How do you feel in the morning when you get up? 52	How do you feel when you finish work? 52
If you didn't have to work, what time would you get up? 52	What do you do first after finishing work? 52
What time do you usually start work? 52	During which part of the day are you at your best? 52
What time of the day would you like to start work? 52	Is there any part of the day you really don't like? 52
What time do you usually get up on weekends? 52	Is there a time of day when you really like to relax and do nothing? 52

53 ● Housework

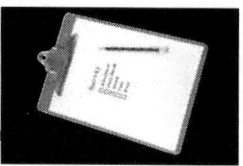

Which of the following housework chores/jobs do you do and how do you feel about them?
Fill in the table then compare and discuss with your partner(s).

✔		Can't do it	Hate doing it	Don't mind doing it	Like doing it
	Washing the dishes by hand				
	Drying the dishes				
	Loading the dishwasher				
	Emptying the dishwasher				
	Washing clothes by hand				
	Loading the washing machine				
	Hanging washing				
	Folding clean laundry				
	Shopping for food				
	Cooking				
	Cleaning up the kitchen				
	General cleaning				
	Tidying up				
	Shopping for household items				
	Ironing				
	Taking the trash out				
	Cleaning the yard/garden				
	Cleaning communal areas of an apartment building/residential area				
	Shoveling snow				
	Raking leaves				
	Repairing clothes				
	Repairing other things				

If you are female, do you use makeup?
If yes, why? If no, why not?

54

What do you think about products
such as anti-aging creams or body lotions?

54

If you are male, do you like to
see women with makeup?
If yes, why? If no, why not?

54

What do you think about:

- piercings?
- tattoos?
- jewelry?

54

Do you think some women use
too much makeup?

54

What do you think about beauty
treatments?

54

What do you think about children and
teenagers using makeup?

54

How much time do you spend on
your hair?

54

What do you think about men using
makeup or other cosmetics?

54

What do you think about plastic surgery?

54

What do you think about cosmetics
companies using animals for testing?

54

Can you think of famous people who
have had plastic surgery?
What do you think of them?

46

55 • Sleep

1. On average, how many hours a night do you sleep:

   During the week?_____

   On weekends?   _____

   55

2. Do you think you get enough sleep?

   55

3. Do you ever sleep too much?

   55

4. What time do you usually go to sleep:

   During the week?_____

   On weekends?   _____

   55

5. When you go to bed, how long does it usually take you to fall asleep?

   55

6. Do you ever get insomnia?
   Have you ever used sleeping tablets?

   55

7. How often during the night do you wake up?

   55

8. How do you usually feel when you wake up in the morning:

   During the week?_____

   On weekends? ·   _____

   55

9. Do you take naps during the day?
   If so, where and for how long?

   55

10. What is your favorite and most productive part of the day?

    ☐ Morning ☐ Afternoon ☐ Evening
    ☐ Night time

    55

11. Do you have any kind of bedtime routine that helps you to sleep?

    55

12. Do you remember your dreams the next day?
    Do you ever have nightmares?

    55

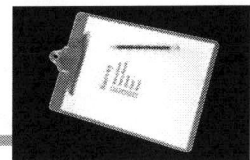

- **Have you heard of the phrase "Big Brother"?**

- **Where does it come from? What does it signify?**

Discuss the following questions with your partner(s).

1. Do you ever think about:
   - how much of your personal information is stored electronically?
   - how much the government knows about you?
   - how much the police know about you?
   - how much your bank/credit card companies know about you?
   - how much your health insurance company knows about you?
   - how much your employer knows about you?
   - how much the internet search engines know about you?

2. When you fill in forms, do you ever wonder why they need to know all this information?

3. Do you ever worry about your privacy?

4. Have you ever experienced an invasion of your privacy?

5. How do you feel about national identification cards?

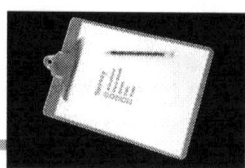

Imagine you have to spend ten years alone on a desert island. There is food and water and some kind of house for you to live in. There are no dangerous animals. The weather is always warm, and you are safe. But you will be alone for ten years without phones, computers, or internet, and no way to contact other people. You are allowed to have ten books, ten music CDs, and ten DVDs of TV shows or movies (you will have a CD player and a DVD player). You can take five items of clothing and two pairs of shoes. You are allowed to bring a musical instrument that you don't know how to play as well as books and DVDs to help you learn how to play it. You are allowed to bring one language course – books and CDs – in order to learn one language that you cannot speak at all at the moment. After ten years you will go back to your country. Answer the questions below and then compare with some partners and discuss your answers.

1. Which ten books would you bring with you?

2. Which ten music CDs would you bring with you?

3. Which ten DVDs would you bring with you?

4. Which five items of clothing would you bring with you?

5. Which two pairs of shoes would you bring with you?

6. Which musical instrument would you bring with you?

7. Which language would you learn?

58 • Immigration

Work through the following questionnaire with your partner(s). Explain your opinions.

1. Western countries need immigration to ensure economic growth.

   ☐ agree strongly   ☐ agree   ☐ not sure/it depends   ☐ disagree   ☐ disagree strongly

2. Immigration is causing a housing crisis in Western countries.

   ☐ agree strongly   ☐ agree   ☐ not sure/it depends   ☐ disagree   ☐ disagree strongly

3. Immigrants do jobs that most Westerners are not willing to do.

   ☐ agree strongly   ☐ agree   ☐ not sure/it depends   ☐ disagree   ☐ disagree strongly

4. Immigrants are willing to work for little money, which is unfair to other workers.

   ☐ agree strongly   ☐ agree   ☐ not sure/it depends   ☐ disagree   ☐ disagree strongly

5. Immigrants usually don't integrate into society, preferring to stay with their own people.
   This often creates ghettos.

   ☐ agree strongly   ☐ agree   ☐ not sure/it depends   ☐ disagree   ☐ disagree strongly

6. America is a country based on immigration and is the strongest country in the world. How
   can immigration be bad?

   ☐ agree strongly   ☐ agree   ☐ not sure/it depends   ☐ disagree   ☐ disagree strongly

7. Immigrants take jobs and housing away from the native population.

   ☐ agree strongly   ☐ agree   ☐ not sure/it depends   ☐ disagree   ☐ disagree strongly

8. Why should people be prevented from seeking a better life for themselves and their families?

   ☐ agree strongly   ☐ agree   ☐ not sure/it depends   ☐ disagree   ☐ disagree strongly

9. Immigrants should stay in their own countries.

   ☐ agree strongly   ☐ agree   ☐ not sure/it depends   ☐ disagree   ☐ disagree strongly

10. Immigrants enrich their host countries with their culture and skills.

   ☐ agree strongly   ☐ agree   ☐ not sure/it depends   ☐ disagree   ☐ disagree strongly

Part 1. Answer the following questions with your partner(s):

- Who assassinated John F. Kennedy?

- Who assassinated Martin Luther King, Jr.?

- Who was the first man to walk on the moon?

- Who carried out the terrorist attacks on September 11, 2001?

- How did Princess Diana die?

- Why is the US government covering up the truth about UFO's?

Part 2. Consider and discuss the following theories:

- John F. Kennedy was assassinated by a group of powerful right-wing people –
  perhaps even the American government.

- There is no reason to believe that James Earl Ray assassinated Martin Luther King, Jr.
  He was just a small-time crook with no reason to shoot King, and after a forced "confession,"
  he claimed he was innocent until he died.

- Americans never landed on the moon. The whole thing was filmed in a film studio.

- The September 11 attacks were carried out by the American government and/or the CIA.

- Princess Diana and her boyfriend, Dodi Al Fayed, were murdered by the British secret service.

- Sightings of UFO's are well-known and proven, but the US government refuses to let the real
  information come out.

Try to think of reasons why people choose to believe these theories.

Do you think it is possible that any of the theories could be true? Why/Why not?

60 • America Today

The United States is a superpower. Many people believe it has mis-used its power. Many people defend the US as a positive force in the world. Which side are you on? Debate the following statements with some partners. In groups of four, two people argue as "antis" and two as "pros."

Anti	Pro
America has no right to get involved in the problems of other countries. It can't even solve its own problems, and there are many.	America should get involved in international problems and use its power to support democracy and human rights.
America only thinks it is a democracy. It is ruled by corporations and money. It can't even choose good leaders.	America is the symbol of freedom and democracy. People get involved in politics and can have an effect.
America thinks it is the world's policeman. It thinks it can solve everything with its superior military. Americans love guns and wars.	Unfortunately, the world needs a country with a strong military force to combat the terrorists and evil leaders who destroy their own people.
It is very sad that the world is becoming more and more Americanized. Americans have no culture. They worship power and money.	America has brought the world great music (jazz, blues, rock and roll), the movie industry, great literature, and huge technological advances.
Huge American corporations exploit workers in poor countries and pollute the environment in many parts of the world. America gets richer and the poor get poorer.	Americans are helping developing countries by importing so many of their needs from other countries. Millions are employed because of the power of the American consumer.

Teacher's Notes

Many of the suggestions for songs to introduce the activities came from my wife, Nuray Sümbültepe Keegan.

1 • In My Opinion

page 3

PROCEDURE: You will need one set of cards for each group of students and copies of the *Useful Phrases* handouts on pages 1 and 2 for each student. First of all, read through the handouts with the students and deal with any questions they have. This will take 5 or 10 minutes or so. Put the students into small groups: pairs, threes, or fours (threes works really well).

Put the cards in a pile, face down. Students take turns taking a card. They read the card to themselves and then have to argue in favor of the opinion that is on the card, regardless of what they personally believe. The other members of the group are free to agree or disagree, whatever they want. The students can refer to the handouts to help them express their opinions and agree/disagree. When the discussion has run its course, the next student takes a card and argues the opinion, and so on. Tell the students that they are not allowed to go through the cards looking for one that they like; they have to take what comes. Note that there are two pages of cards.

TIME: 45-60 minutes, if all the cards are used

THINGS TO LOOK OUT FOR: Some students find it very hard to argue something that they don't actually believe. The clearer you make your instructions, the less likely this is to occur. Giving a clear demo of how to argue the opinion is a good idea, otherwise some students will simply pick up the card and read it as it is, rather than argue in favor of the opinion.

POTENTIALLY DIFFICULT WORDS AND EXPRESSIONS: homosexual, heterosexual, compulsory military service, unemployed, materialistic, influence, euthanasia, religious, banned

2 • I think . . .

page 5

For a shorter, easier discussion, use only the first 12 questions on the questionnaire.

PROCEDURE: Give out the appropriate questionnaire and tell the students to go through all the questions one at a time, explaining their answers to their partners.

TIME: From 45 to 90 minutes, depending on how open and communicative the students are and how many questions you decide to work on

THINGS TO LOOK OUT FOR: Some of the questions are rather personal, which some students are not comfortable with. I always tell them they don't have to answer any questions they don't like.

POTENTIALLY DIFFICULT WORDS: fear, to admire, proud, to lie, to relax, depressed, talent, extravagance, regret

3 • What do you think?

page 6

PROCEDURE: Write a word on the board which could be the topic of a discussion, e.g. Sports or Politics. Elicit from the students some questions which they could ask their partners if they were told they had to discuss these topics. Note that there are two pages of cards.

You will need one set of cards for each group of students. Put the students into small groups: pairs, threes, or fours. Put the cards face down. Students take turns to pick up a card and ask their partners any questions they want on the topic. It is of course desirable if a discussion develops, and follow-up questions are to be encouraged.

When the discussion has run out of steam, the next student takes a card and asks a question, and so on. Tell the students that they are not allowed to go through the cards looking for one that they like; they have to take what comes.

TIME: From 45 minutes to several hours

THINGS TO LOOK OUT FOR: Make your instructions absolutely clear, i.e. the students are supposed to initiate a discussion by asking a question, otherwise the first student will pick up a card and read it as it is, e.g. "Ask your partners about films." This is not what you want.

4 • Have you ever . . .

page 8

You could begin this activity by playing the song **Have You Ever Been in Love?** *by Celine Dionne.*

PROCEDURE: Write a question on the board with the present perfect and "ever," e.g. "Have you ever broken a bone in your body?" Elicit the two possible answers of "Yes, I have" and "No, I haven't." Elicit or explain that, if someone wants to give more information when they answer "yes," they have to change tense, e.g. "Last year I broke my arm."

Point out that the "have you ever" construction means at any point in your life up till now, but the detailed answer needs to be in the simple past as we are giving specific information about a past event. Give out the handout and ask the students to answer the yes/no questions alone.

Put the students into groups of two, three, or four. For every question to which they have answered "yes" they have to tell their partners the story of what happened, using, of course, the simple past.

TIME: 30-45 minutes

POTENTIALLY DIFFICULT WORDS AND EXPRESSIONS: Valuable, to break a law, to fail/pass an exam, to lose your temper, to fall in love at first sight, to break someone's heart, the opposite sex.

5 • Annoying Habits

page 9

PROCEDURE: Give out the handout. Go through the phrases which can be used to express annoyance.

Put the students into small groups and tell them to go through the questionnaire, discussing the reasons for their answers with each other. Do a class summary, asking the students to decide what is the one most annoying habit people have.

You can also ask them two additional questions:
- Ask them to try to guess which habits of theirs are annoying to you.
- Which habits of teachers annoy them?

TIME: 15-30 minutes

POTENTIALLY DIFFICULT WORDS AND EXPRESSIONS: to blow one's nose, to burp, to show off, to yawn, to interrupt

6 • Are you a communicator?

page 10

*You could begin this activity by playing the song **Communication** by Spandau Ballet.*

PROCEDURE: Give out the handout and tell the students to complete it first alone. Put the students into pairs or small groups. They should go through the questionnaire, explaining their answers.

When the discussions are finished, tell the students to add up their score as follows:

> *Each 'often' scores 2 points*
> *Each 'sometimes' scores 1 point*
> *Each 'rarely' scores 0 points*
> *Each 'never' scores minus 1 point (i.e. they have to deduct 1 point).*

The solution is as follows:

> 18-24 points means you are a first-class communicator!
> 10-17 points means you are a good communicator, but you can enjoy your own company too.
> Under 10 points means you are more introverted and probably enjoy being alone.

It is important to point out that there is nothing good or bad about this. Some people are more communicative than others and the less openly communicative people probably have other skills.

TIME: 10-20 minutes

POTENTIALLY DIFFICULT WORDS AND EXPRESSIONS: to pay compliments, a crowd, advice

7 • Computers

page 11

You could begin this activity by playing **Computer Song** *by Jim Noir.*

PROCEDURE: Divide the students into groups of two if possible. Give out both pages of the handout. The students should interview each other, making notes about their partners' habits. When they are finished, they can compare and discuss their answers. A further activity could be to report back to the class or to another group about their partners' computer/internet activities.

TIME: From 20 to 45 minutes, depending on how interested the students are

THINGS TO LOOK OUT FOR: If your students don't use or have no access to computers this activity won't work. Otherwise, it is usually very lively.

POTENTIALLY DIFFICULT WORDS AND EXPRESSIONS: chatting (online chatting), online services, on average, a waste of time, experiences, addiction, to imagine

8 • How green are you?

page 13

You could begin (or follow up) this activity by playing the song **Radium Rain** *by Bruce Cockburn. This activity was inspired by Al Gore's film* **An Inconvenient Truth**.

PROCEDURE: Give out the questionnaire. The students check all the answers that apply; for example, if they sometimes go to work by car and sometimes by bicycle, they check both of those. After the discussion, give out or explain the key (page 14) and maybe have an all-class discussion. An excellent follow-up activity is to watch Al Gore's film.

TIME: From 20 to 45 minutes

THINGS TO LOOK OUT FOR: This is potentially quite controversial, as some people continue to believe that human activity is not causing global warming.

POTENTIALLY DIFFICULT WORDS AND EXPRESSIONS: compost, reusable, renewable energy, (household) appliances

9 • Clothes

page 15

You could begin this activity by playing the song **Fashion** *by David Bowie or the song of the same title (though it is a different song) by Lady Gaga.*

PROCEDURE: It might be an idea to pre-teach some vocabulary relating to this topic, such as fashionable, to look smart, to dress casually, designer, and so on. Point out that 'clothes' also includes shoes. Divide the students into groups of two or three. Give out the cards. Note that there are two pages of cards.

The students should go through the questions, giving and discussing their answers.

TIME: From 20 to 45 minutes, depending on how interested the students are and how many cards you use

THINGS TO LOOK OUT FOR: Some students (especially males) are just not interested in this topic.

POTENTIALLY DIFFICULT WORDS AND EXPRESSIONS: special occasions, traditional/national costume, uniform, role models, clothes designer

10 • Shoes

page 17

PROCEDURE: Put the students into pairs or small groups and let them discuss their answers to the questions. You can do a whole class round up at the end. If possible, it is good to have a mix of male and female students in each group as their answers tend to vary quite a lot.

TIME: 15-30 minutes.

THINGS TO LOOK OUT FOR: This topic will not be of interest to all students. Knowledge of the second conditional (If I had……/I would …..) is necessary for this activity.

POTENTIALLY DIFFICULT WORDS: Character, personality, expensive, approximately.

11 • Dreams

page 18

There is an old Everly Brothers song called Dream, Dream, Dream *which would make a nice introduction to this activity. Supertramp also have a great song called* Dreamer *which would also fit well. Another idea would be to download from the internet a video clip of Martin Luther King's famous 'I have a dream' speech and use that as either a warmer or a follow up to this activity.*

This activity can be combined with and followed by Activity 11, "Reality."

PROCEDURE: Put the students into small groups of two or three. You need a copy of the handout for each student.

The students go through the "Dreams" handout, discussing their answers. Question 7 is only for students who are interested in a team sport such as soccer. (You might want to point out that "soccer" is American, Australian, and Irish English for "football.")

"Reality" Option: When the students are ready, give out the "Reality" handout.
The students should fill it in alone first of all and then discuss their answers with their partners, explaining why they have graded the questions as they have. When they are ready, give out, or read aloud, the solution on page 19.

TIME: From 15 to 20 minutes

POTENTIALLY DIFFICULT WORDS: weight, height

12 • Getting the News

page 19

You could begin this activity by playing the song **A Day in the Life** *by The Beatles.*

PROCEDURE: Put the students into groups of two, three, or four. Give out the questionnaire, one per student, and ask the students to go through it. They should then compare and discuss their answers with their partners.

Bring the class together for a general discussion at the end. With multi-national groups it can be very interesting to ask which is the most reliable and objective news service available to them, and to go into the question of whether we can believe what we are told or not. You can also ask them what is more important to them: international, national, or regional news. If you are teaching international students in an English-speaking country, you can also ask them what they think of the news service in the country they are in.

TIME: 15-30 minutes

THINGS TO LOOK OUT FOR: Make sure the students realize that the topic is the news and not TV or radio in general.

With multi-national groups you may have students who have no experience of independent news providers. This could be tricky. There are also some people who are absolutely not interested in this topic, so consider your group carefully when using this activity.

POTENTIALLY DIFFICULT WORDS: blogs, chat, colleagues

13 • Animals, Meat, Vegetarianism

page 20

You could begin this activity by playing **The Animal Song** *by Savage Garden. An alternative would be the controversial and highly emotional song* **Meat is Murder** *by The Smiths.*

PROCEDURE: Put the students into groups of two, three, or four. Give out the questionnaire, one per student or per group, and ask the students to go through it.

Bring the groups together for an all-class discussion at the end.

TIME: 15-40 minutes, very variable

THINGS TO LOOK OUT FOR: Some students may have no concept of animal rights, so be prepared for this. There is also the potential for conflict (and/or great discussion) between vegetarians and diehard meat eaters.

POTENTIALLY DIFFICULT WORDS AND EXPRESSIONS: pets, to annoy, vegetarianism, animal rights, fur, leather

14 • Emotions

page 21

You could begin this activity by playing the song **Emotions** *by Mariah Carey or, (and in my opinion infinitely superior),* **Mixed Emotions** *by The Rolling Stones.*

PROCEDURE: Give out a copy of the questionnaire to each student. Go through the introductory paragraph with the whole group, and have a class discussion about whether the stereotypes mentioned are true or not.

Ask the students to complete the questionnaire alone. They should then get into small groups – pairs, threes, or fours (threes works really well). They should then explain the reasons for their answers to each other.

When they have finished their discussions, tell them to calculate their score as follows:

> Each 'agree' = 0 points
> Each 'disagree' = 2 points
> Each 'it depends' = 1 point.

The key is as follows:

> 17-24 points means you are very open about your emotions.
> 10-16 points means you have a good balance between being open about your emotions and keeping your emotions under control.
> Under 10 points means you really like to keep a stiff upper lip in public.

Tell the students that there is no right or wrong way to be in this respect. Being more open emotionally is not necessarily better than being less open; it is just different.

TIME: 20-30 minutes

THINGS TO LOOK OUT FOR: I suppose it is possible that you will have students who have never heard of John Lennon or Princess Diana. In this case you may need to explain who they were and that when they died people did indeed openly weep in the street.

POTENTIALLY DIFFICULT WORDS AND EXPRESSIONS: embarrassing, passionately, to argue, spouse, to disturb, ridiculous, to be attracted to, sentimental

15 • Friendship

page 22

A really good way to introduce this activity is to play **You've Got a Friend** *by Carole King (James Taylor also recorded a fabulous version). There is also* **That's What Friends Are For**, *recorded by many, but Dionne Warwick's version is really great.*

PROCEDURE: Divide the students into groups of two or three. Give out the cards, one set per group.

The students should go through the questions, giving and discussing their answers. They will very likely need quite a lot of help from you regarding vocabulary, and you will have excellent opportunities for vocabulary input during this activity.

TIME: 20-30 minutes

POTENTIALLY DIFFICULT WORDS: qualities (in a person), to value, to prefer

16 • Gays and Lesbians

 *page 24*

PROCEDURE: Divide the students into groups of two or three. Give out the first page of the handout. First, check that the students understand the head-words at the top. Ask the students to go through the questions in their groups, giving and discussing their answers. Give out the handout on the second page when the students are ready.

TIME: From 20 to 45 minutes

THINGS TO LOOK OUT FOR: This is a very sensitive topic and is not suitable for all students and classes. Make sure that your students can deal with this topic before attempting this activity.

If students wish to answer with "it depends," they need to explain on what it depends.

POTENTIALLY DIFFICULT WORDS AND EXPRESSIONS: gay, lesbian, homosexual, homosexuality, homophobic, homophobia, sexual orientation, to keep to yourself, genetic

17 • Men, Women, Husbands, Wives

 *page 25*

You could begin this activity by playing the song **Women and Men** *by They Might Be Giants or, of course,* **Stand by Your Man** *by Tammy Wynette.*

PROCEDURE: Put the students into groups of three or four, ideally with a gender mix. Give out the questionnaire and ask the students to discuss the statements. Bring the class together for a roundup, general discussion about roles of men and women, women's rights, etc.

TIME: From 20 to 40 minutes, depending on how heated the discussions become

THINGS TO LOOK OUT FOR: Some of the statements are deliberately provocative and may cause some offense. They may also cause good discussion. For statement 15, you might want to point out that statistically women drivers cause far fewer accidents than male drivers.

POTENTIALLY DIFFICULT WORDS AND EXPRESSIONS: to share, successful, to have the last word, to manage money, efficient, emotional reactions, intuitive, relationship

18 • Family

 *page 26*

PROCEDURE: Playing the song 'We are Family' by Sister Sledge would be a great way to introduce this topic. Put the students into pairs or small groups and let them discuss their answers to the questions. You can do a whole class round up at the end.

TIME: 15-30 minutes.

THINGS TO LOOK OUT FOR: Some students may find this topic too personal, especially if they have serious issues with their family.

POTENTIALLY DIFFICULT WORDS: Immediate/extended family, head of the family.

19 • Languages

page 27

PROCEDURE: Put the students into groups of two, three, or four. Give out the cards, one set per group, and ask the students to go through the questions. Bring the class together for a summary/general discussion at the end.

TIME: 15-25 minutes

POTENTIALLY DIFFICULT WORDS AND EXPRESSIONS: dialect, mother tongue, acceptable, common.

20 • Life Choices

page 28

PROCEDURE: The first version is for people who work; the second version is for full-time students. If you have a mixed group, you can give each student the relevant version. For a group who are all employed, you can combine this unit quite successfully with the following unit on work.

Put the students into groups of two, three, or four. Give out the questionnaire, one per student, and ask the students to go through it.

TIME: 15 -25 minutes

THINGS TO LOOK OUT FOR: Students need to be able to use the imaginative conditional (If I had.......I would...) for this unit.

POTENTIALLY DIFFICULT WORDS AND EXPRESSIONS: order of importance, close relationship, according to

21 • Work

page 29

You can combine this activity with the previous activity quite successfully.

There are various songs on the topic of work that you could use to get this activity going. For example, **Working Man** *by* *Rush,* **Working for the Man** *by Roy Orbison,* **9 to 5** *by Dolly Parton,* **Working at the Factory** *by the Kinks, and there are doubtless many more.*

PROCEDURE: Put the students into groups of two, three, or four. Give out the worksheet, one per student, and ask the students to go through it.

TIME: 10-20 minutes

THINGS TO LOOK OUT FOR: This activity works only for people who are working.

If you are teaching people from the same company, some people might not like discussing this in front of their colleagues. On the other hand, it can also be very cathartic for such people to do this activity.

Students need to be able to use the imaginative conditional (If I had.......I would...) for this unit.

For the final question, the results of the survey were that people had no sense of direction, felt useless, and had no reason to get up in the morning.

POTENTIALLY DIFFICULT WORDS AND EXPRESSIONS: lottery jackpot, challenging, frustrating, rewarding, tedious, interesting, exciting, repetitive, satisfying

22 • Vacations

page 30

PROCEDURE: You could introduce this unit by playing the old Cliff Richard song, 'Summer Holiday'.
Give out the handout and ask the students to fill in the tables alone. Then in pairs or small groups they exchange their experiences and answer the questions that follow the tables.

Finish with a whole class round up.

TIME: 15-30 minutes

POTENTIALLY DIFFICULT WORDS: Depending on where you are teaching, you may need to point out the difference between vacation (American English) and Holiday (UK English).

23 • How Do You Relax

page 30

PROCEDURE: Give out the handout and ask the students to fill in which relaxation activities they do. Obviously there may be activities that they do both alone and with others and it is OK to tick both boxes.

After filling in the table, they compare and discuss with other students in small groups. It is nice to change the groupings while they are doing it so that they talk to different students.

TIME: 15-25 minutes

POTENTIALLY DIFFICULT WORDS: Puzzle, diary, journal, gambling, stock market

24 • Insurance

page 32

A great way to begin this activity is to play the classic Status Quo song **You're in the Army Now**.

PROCEDURE: Put the students into groups of two, three, or four. Give out the questionnaire, one per student, and

TIME: 15-25 minutes

POTENTIALLY DIFFICULT WORDS: Puzzle, diary, journal, gambling, stock market

25 • Military Service

page 33

A great way to begin this activity is to play the classic Status Quo song **You're in the Army Now.**

PROCEDURE: Put the students into groups of two, three, or four. Give out the questionnaire, one per student, and ask the students to go through it. Bring the groups together for an all-class discussion at the end. With multi-national groups it can be very interesting to ask about the situation in their countries, whether they think military service is necessary, and if yes, whether both women and men should do it.

TIME: 15-30 minutes, very variable

THINGS TO LOOK OUT FOR: With multi-national groups you may be confronted with students who have no experience of military service. Most native English speaking teachers also have no experience of military service, which some students find quite interesting.

POTENTIALLY DIFFICULT WORDS AND EXPRESSIONS: citizen, defend, homeland, compulsory, to ensure, to have the right, conscientious objector, purpose, slavery, violation, keen, to be drafted, experience, in favor of

26 • Money

page 34

A great way to begin this activity would be to play **Money, Money, Money** *by Abba, or the old classic* **Money** *by, among others, The Beatles, or my favorite,* **Money** *by Pink Floyd. (Or, for that matter, all of the above).*

PROCEDURE: Put the students into small groups, three being an ideal number. Give out the questionnaire, one per student. Students go through the questionnaire alone first, then, in their groups, they explain to each other to what extent each statement is true for them.

TIME: 15-30 minutes

POTENTIALLY DIFFICULT WORDS: jealous, behavior, poverty, in debt, to gamble, to lend, to borrow

27 • Music

page 35

One way to start this activity is to play a song or a piece of music that you really like and just ask the students what they think of it. Alternatively, play a piece of music you really dislike. You can also play a variety of short pieces of music and ask the students to close their eyes and listen to each one and then write down their feelings and reactions, which they should do after each piece you play, and then compare and discuss with partners.

Or you can just go straight into it.

PROCEDURE: Divide the students into groups of two or three. Give out the cards, one set per group. The students should go through the questions, giving and discussing their answers. They may well need your help with vocabulary, so be prepared to input. Note that there are two pages of cards.

TIME: There are two pages of cards, so this activity could be done on two occasions, each taking 15-45 minutes.

POTENTIALLY DIFFICULT WORDS AND EXPRESSIONS: nowadays, all-time favorite, taste in music, to get on your nerves, fascinated by, to read music

28 • Names

page 37

You could begin this activity by reading from Shakespeare's **Romeo and Juliet**, *specifically Juliet's speech, which begins "What's in a name?"*

PROCEDURE: Divide the students into groups of two or three. Give out the handout, one per student. The students should fill in the names. It is OK if they can't think of a name for every section.

TIME: 10-45 minutes, extremely variable

THINGS TO LOOK OUT FOR: Some students find this activity too personal; the teacher should be sensitive to this.

POTENTIALLY DIFFICULT WORDS: influenced, to admire

29 • Patriotism

page 35

An interesting way to start this lesson is to play John Lennon's **Imagine** *and to ask students what they think it is about, especially the verse which begins "Imagine there's no countries."*

PROCEDURE: As a warm-up, ask the students what they understand by the following words, and if they have a positive or a negative connotation:

- A patriot, patriotic, patriotism
- A nationalist, nationalistic, nationalism

Divide them into small groups and give out the cards. If you can mix nationalities, all the better. The students should go through the questions, discussing their answers.

Do a class summary at the end. I find the students like to hear my opinions about my nationality and how I feel about my own and other countries.

With the right mix of students, I also like to have a class discussion about whether jokes about other nations are just fun or whether there is a racist element.

TIME: 20-40 minutes

THINGS TO LOOK OUT FOR: This is a sensitive area to touch on and you could be opening a can of worms, so be sure your students can deal with the topic before attempting this activity.

30 • Politics

 *page 39*

*You could begin this activity by playing the song **Political** by Spirit of the West. This song is not actually about politics but the text of the chorus would introduce the topic rather well. Otherwise, there are many protest songs you could use including classics like **Blowing in the Wind** or **The Times They Are A-Changin'** by Bob Dylan or **Imagine** by John Lennon.*

PROCEDURE: Put the students into groups of two, three, or four. Give out the cards. Have the students give and discuss their answers.

Do a class summary at the end. I find the students like to hear my opinions on this subject.

TIME: 15-30 minutes, depending on how interested in politics the students are

THINGS TO LOOK OUT FOR: Students need to able to use the imaginative conditional (If I were…I would…) for this activity.

This is a sensitive area to touch, so be sure your students can deal with the topic before attempting this activity. Some people are also completely turned off by the whole topic of politics; this activity can fall flat if the group is just not into it.

POTENTIALLY DIFFICULT WORDS AND EXPRESSIONS: head of state, figurehead, to vote, to be/get elected, political system, political party, scandal, politician, to be in power, ethnic minorities

31 • Rituals and Traditions

 *page 40*

This activity provides excellent opportunities to practice past tenses, especially the simple past.

PROCEDURE: Divide the students into groups of two or three. Give out the cards. The students should go through the questions, giving and discussing their answers.

TIME: From 20 to 60 minutes; very variable. The first question alone can sometimes take up an entire lesson.

POTENTIALLY DIFFICULT WORDS AND EXPRESSIONS: rituals, traditions, special/religious meaning, to practice a ritual, to die out, memory

32 • The Death Penalty

 *page 41*

*You could begin this activity by playing the song **Let him Dangle** by Elvis Costello. It is a great song which tells a true story, but the text has some quite complicated language, So it would probably only be appropriate with a more advanced group. You could, of course, also follow up this activity by looking at this song.*

PROCEDURE: Divide the students into groups of two or three. Give out the handout, one per student. The students should go through the questions, giving and discussing their answers.

TIME: 10-30 minutes, very variable

THINGS TO LOOK OUT FOR: Students may have hugely varying reactions to this topic, usually depending on their country/culture of origin. For some, the death penalty is an everyday fact of life (e.g. in China and some Arab countries), whereas Western Europeans are frequently vehemently opposed to the death penalty. Great discussion can ensue as a result.

POTENTIALLY DIFFICULT WORDS AND EXPRESSIONS: death penalty, deterrent, serious crimes, to deserve to die, cruel and inhuman punishment, violence, to be treated (well or badly), murder victim, justice, immoral

33 • Religion  *page 42*

PROCEDURE: Divide the students into groups of two or three. Give out the cards. The students should go through the questions, giving and discussing their answers. They may need quite a lot of help from you with the vocabulary.

TIME: 10-45 minutes, very variable

THINGS TO LOOK OUT FOR: A potentially explosive topic, so be careful with this one. I have had students, for example from some Muslim countries, who are completely shocked at the idea of atheism. On the other hand, I really don't think it does them any harm to be exposed to this concept.

    • *Some students may also find this activity too personal; the teacher should be sensitive to this.*

POTENTIALLY DIFFICULT WORDS AND EXPRESSIONS: religion, religious, atheist, atheism, to pay lip service to, according to the rules, to appear to be, minority, forbidden, conflict

34 • Ethics  *page 43*

This unit was directly inspired by a unit in Gillian Porter-Ladousse's wonderful book, Speaking Personally

PROCEDURE: The students should work through the questionnaire alone first of all, choosing their answers on the basis that they will never get caught or get into trouble if they choose a dishonest option.

Then their compare their answers in groups (group of three works well for this activity) and give reasons for their answers. You can change the make up of the groups during the discussion if you want.

At the end, you can do a class round up/discussion. Then tell them there is a key: 2 points for an A answer, 0 points for a B and minus 1 point for a C. They can calculate their score and see who is the most honest person in the group.

TIME: 25-40 minutes.

THINGS TO LOOK OUT FOR: Make your instructions absolutely clear, i.e. the students have to choose their answer based on the principle that they will never get into trouble whatever answer they choose. We don't want students saying "if I chose C, I would be in a lot of trouble if I got caught". They will never get caught.

The students need to be familiar with the second conditional (If I had..../I would take....) so it is a good idea to review this before doing this unit.

POTENTIALLY DIFFICULT WORDS AND EXPRESSIONS: religion, religious, atheist, atheism, to pay lip service to, according to the rules, to appear to be, minority, forbidden, conflict

35 • School  *page 44*

*You could begin this activity by playing the song **Another Brick in the Wall** by Pink Floyd or **School** by Supertramp or, to go even further back in time (circa 1971 in fact), Alice Cooper's fantastic **School's Out**.*

There are two versions of this activity: one for those who have left school and one for those still in school. This activity provides excellent opportunities to practice simple past and present tenses.

PROCEDURE: Put the students into groups of two, three, or four. Give out the cards, one per student or group, and ask the students to go through the questions. Bring the class together for a summary/general discussion at the end. With multi-national groups it can be very interesting to ask about the situation in their countries. Note that there are two pages of cards.

TIME: 15-40 minutes, very variable

POTENTIALLY DIFFICULT WORDS AND EXPRESSIONS: subject (school subject), special focus, bullying, salary

36 • Smoking   *page 46*

It is possible to combine this activity with the next two units on alcohol and drugs, making a long unit on addiction.

PROCEDURE: Put the students into groups of two, three, or four. Give out the questionnaire, one per student, and ask the students to go through it. After this opening discussion, give out the cards and have the students discuss them.

Bring the class together for a summary, general discussion at the end. With multi-national groups it can be very interesting to ask about the situation in their countries regarding acceptance of smoking, provision of non-smoking areas, smoking bans, and so on.

TIME: 15-40 minutes, very variable

THINGS TO LOOK OUT FOR: Potentially a controversial topic, but most people have opinions on this topic, and great discussions can develop.

POTENTIALLY DIFFICULT WORDS AND EXPRESSIONS: physically, mentally, evidence, unhealthy effects, to give up, to put pressure on someone, to bother, to ban/be banned, to breathe, to encourage, to damage (health), to compensate

37 • Drinking

 *page 48*

You could begin this activity by playing the song **Have a Drink on Me** *by AC/DC if you think your students can cope with it. There is also the old classic* **Little Old Wine Drinker Me** *by Dean Martin.*

It is possible to combine this activity with the two units on smoking and drugs to make a long unit on the topic of addiction.

PROCEDURE: Put the students into groups of two, three, or four. Give out the table, one per student, and ask the students to go through it and then compare and discuss with partners. Bring the groups together for an all-class discussion at the end. With multi-national groups it can be very interesting to ask about the situation in their countries regarding acceptance of alcohol.

TIME: For just this activity, 10-20 minutes

THINGS TO LOOK OUT FOR: Potentially a controversial topic, especially if there are strict Muslims in your class. On the other hand, they are usually aware that other people drink alcohol, and good discussions can develop as a result.

This activity is only suitable for people of legal drinking age.

POTENTIALLY DIFFICULT WORDS AND EXPRESSIONS: to recommend, alcohol unit, relevant, to relax, stress, to celebrate, bored, shy, to be addicted to, drunk

38 • Drugs

 *page 49*

You could start this activity by playing **The Drugs Don't Work** *by The Verve.*

It is possible to combine this activity with the two units on smoking and drinking to make a long unit on the topic of addiction.

PROCEDURE: Put the students into groups of two, three, or four. Give out the cards, one per student or per group, and ask the students to go through them and discuss their answers.

Bring the class together for a summary, general discussion at the end. With multi-national groups it can be very interesting to ask about the situation in their countries regarding acceptance of drugs.

TIME: For just this activity, 10-20 minutes

THINGS TO LOOK OUT FOR: An extremely controversial topic, so make sure your students can deal with it before attempting this. On the other hand, the questions are designed so that no one has to admit that they take or have ever taken any illegal drugs. It is up to them if they choose to do so.

POTENTIALLY DIFFICULT WORDS AND EXPRESSIONS: to be legalized, to control, effectively, to tax, soft drugs, hard drugs, to experiment, strict (laws), to escape from (a boring life), weak

39 • Sports

page 50

*There are probably a lot of songs you could use to introduce this activity but **We are the Champions** by Queen comes particularly to mind.*

PROCEDURE: Put the students into groups of two, three, or four. Give out the cards, one set per group, and ask the students to go through them and discuss their answers. Bring the class together for a summary general discussion at the end.

TIME: 10-40 minutes, depending on how interested in this topic the learners are

THINGS TO LOOK OUT FOR: There are people (apparently) who are completely uninterested in sports, so this activity will not be of interest to them.

POTENTIALLY DIFFICULT WORDS AND EXPRESSIONS: spectator, top sports people, professional, competition

340 • Time

page 47

*This unit was entirely inspired by the marvelous Pink Floyd song **Time**. You could of course play this song as an intro to this activity.*

PROCEDURE: Put the students into groups of two, three, or four. Give out the cards, one set per group, and ask the students to go through the questions and discuss their answers.

Bring the class together for a summary general discussion at the end.

TIME: 10-20 minutes

THINGS TO LOOK FOR: This unit is a bit abstract and philosophical and won't work with every group. With some groups, however, you can be busy for ages.

POTENTIALLY DIFFICULT WORDS AND EXPRESSIONS: actually, to waste time, to have regrets, to spend time, boredom

41 • Technology

page 52

*You could begin this activity by playing the song **Welcome to the Machine** by Pink Floyd.*

PROCEDURE: Put the students into groups of two, three, or four. Give out the cards, one set per group, and ask the students to go through the questions. Bring the groups together for an all-class discussion at the end. With multi-national groups it can be very interesting to ask about the situation in their countries.

TIME: 10-20 minutes

THINGS TO LOOK OUT FOR: You may get some "technophobe" students who hate technology, but even then there is plenty to discuss as to why they hate it.

POTENTIALLY DIFFICULT WORDS AND EXPRESSIONS: disadvantages, to live without, frustrated, to repair

42 • Smart Phones

page 53

PROCEDURE: Give out the handout and ask the students to fill in the table. They should then compare and discuss with a partner to two. When they have finished, they can answer the discussion questions in groups. You can do a whole class round up at the end.

TIME: 15-25 minutes

THINGS TO LOOK OUT FOR: If some students don't own a smart phone, this activity won't work. Question two and three require an understanding of the present perfect.

POTENTIALLY DIFFICULT WORDS: Timetables, puzzles, to edit videos/photos

43 • Social Media

page 54

PROCEDURE: Introduce the topic of social media – you can elicit the names of well-known social media sites or show some visuals.

TIME: 10-20 minutes

THINGS TO LOOK OUT FOR: If your students don't use social media (apparently such people do exist) this activity won't be interesting for them.

POTENTIALLY DIFFICULT WORDS: To pass the time, current events, to network, to promote

44 • Socializing

page 55

PROCEDURE: Give out the handout and ask the students to fill in which social activities they do with friends, family and alone. Obviously there may be activities that they do only with friends but some activities they may do with friends, with family and alone. They don't have to choose between these, they can tick every box.

After filling in the table, they compare and discuss with other students in small groups. It is nice to change the groupings while they are doing it so that they talk to different students.

TIME: 15-25 minutes

THINGS TO LOOK OUT FOR: Students who don't socialize a lot might not have much to say.

POTENTIALLY DIFFICULT WORDS: Nature reserve, botanical gardens, art exhibition, religious ceremony/ritual

45 • Transportation

 page 56

You could begin this activity by playing the song **Traffic Jam** *by James Taylor.*

PROCEDURE: Put the students into groups of two, three, or four. Give out the questionnaire, one per student, and ask the students to go through it and discuss their answers. Bring the groups together for an all-class discussion at the end.

TIME: 10-20 minutes

THINGS TO LOOK OUT FOR: Most people have opinions on this topic, but some learners may find it a bit dull.

POTENTIALLY DIFFICULT WORDS AND EXPRESSIONS: place of work/study, relevant, efficient, public transportation

46 • Reading

 page 57

PROCEDURE: Put the students into groups of two, three, or four. Give out the questionnaire, one per student, and ask the students to go through it and discuss their answers. Bring the groups together for an all-class discussion at the end.

TIME: 10-20 minutes

THINGS TO LOOK OUT FOR: Some people will swear that they never read, but filling in the table should show them that this is simply not true.

POTENTIALLY DIFFICULT WORDS AND EXPRESSIONS: fiction, non-fiction, instruction/technical manuals, text messages, subtitles, advertising slogans, recipes, bumper stickers

47 • Television

  page 59

You could begin this activity by playing the song **Video Killed the Radio Star** *by The Buggles.*

PROCEDURE: Put the students into groups of two, three, or four. Point out that we are specifically dealing with TV programs and not films, which is a separate unit.

Give out the first page of the questionnaire, one per student, and ask the students to fill it out and then compare their answers with their partner(s), or to interview each other and fill in the table for their partner(s).

Give out the second page, if you think it is useful, and have the students speculate about the comments, using "could be" or "must be."

Give out the cards and ask the students to discuss their answers.

Bring the groups together for an all-class discussion at the end.

TIME: From 20 to 45 minutes

THINGS TO LOOK OUT FOR: You may occasionally have students who never watch or have no access to TV, but this is pretty rare. Most people have lively opinions on this topic.

POTENTIALLY DIFFICULT WORDS AND EXPRESSIONS: sitcoms, soaps (soap operas), documentaries, reality shows, fake laughter

48 • Movies

page 62

You could begin this activity by playing the song **Everyone's Gone to the Movies** *by Steely Dan.*

PROCEDURE: You may want to start by pointing out an important difference between British and North American usage, namely that the British watch films in a cinema but North Americans watch movies in a movie theater.

Put the students into groups of two, three, or four. Give out the cards, one set per group, and ask the students to go through them and discuss their answers.

Bring the class together for an all-class discussion at the end.

TIME: 10-20 minutes

THINGS TO LOOK OUT FOR: You may need to pre-teach movie types, such as romantic comedies, dramas, action movies, documentaries, etc.

Some people are not really interested in movies, but this is pretty rare.

POTENTIALLY DIFFICULT WORDS AND EXPRESSIONS: favorite, to prefer, blockbuster movies, a movie industry, movie awards

49 • Food

page 63

There cannot be many more universal topics than this. You can also combine this activity with the unit on beverages and/or drinking.

There are many songs you could use to introduce this activity. Here are a few suggestions: **Breakfast in America** *by* Supertramp, **Food Glorious Food** *from the musical* **Oliver**, **Hungry Heart** *by Bruce Springsteen,* **Life is a Minestrone** *by 10cc,* **Savoy Truffle** *by The Beatles.*

It is important to point out that the English word "kitchen" refers only to the room where food is prepared and is not used to describe a nation's typical food. In English, we usually use the French word "cuisine" or simply "food" to refer to what people eat, for example: "Turkish cuisine" or "Irish food."

PROCEDURE: Put the students into groups of three or four. Give out the questionnaire, one per student, and ask the students to go through the questions, giving and discussing their answers. Then give out the cards, one set per group.

Bring the groups together for an all-class general discussion at the end if appropriate.

TIME: With a mono-lingual group, around 20 to 30 minutes. Much longer (and much more fun) with a multi-national group.

THINGS TO LOOK OUT FOR: People can be quite nationalistic about food and get quite upset if people criticize their country's cuisine.

For the first part, it is good to point out the difference between "I have eaten……..today" and "I ate……….. yesterday" (i.e. today is not finished and I could eat more before the day ends).

Make sure the learners know that "chef" is someone who cooks and does not mean "boss." You might want to point out the difference between "chef" and "cook."

POTENTIALLY DIFFICULT WORDS: healthy, typical, snack

50 • Popular Beverages

page 65

You can combine this activity with the unit on food and/or alcohol.
It is important to point out that this unit is specifically about non-alcoholic drinks.

You could begin this activity by playing the song **One More Cup of Coffee** *by Bob Dylan, or* **Penny Royal** *by Nirvana (I strongly recommend the unplugged version).*

PROCEDURE: Put the students into pairs. Give out the questionnaire, one per student, and ask the students to go through the questions, interviewing each other and making notes. If they want to know what is meant by "details," it should be, for example, what kind of cola, with ice or not, and so on. Bring the groups together for an all-class discussion at the end, if appropriate.

TIME: 10-20 minutes

THINGS TO LOOK OUT FOR: This activity provides a lot of practice of simple present question forms and short answers, so make sure the students are OK with this.

POTENTIALLY DIFFICULT WORDS AND EXPRESSIONS: tap water, mineral water, soft drinks, energy drinks

51 • Medicine and Health Care

page 66

You can combine this activity with the units on food and/or sports.

You could begin by talking about the fact that over 40 million working Americans have no health insurance.

You could begin this activity by playing the song **Bad Case of Loving You** *by Robert Palmer, or* **Doctor, Doctor** *by Iron Maiden.*

PROCEDURE: Put the students into pairs or groups. Give out the cards, one set per group, and ask the students to go through the questions. Finally, bring the groups together for an all-class discussion at the end, if appropriate.

TIME: 10-20 minutes

THINGS TO LOOK OUT FOR: This topic won't be of interest to everyone, but it can provoke great discussions with the right group.

POTENTIALLY DIFFICULT WORDS AND EXPRESSIONS: on average, medical insurance, in respect of, health insurance, to be insured, Western medicine, alternative medicine, pain killers, non-prescription drugs, to take care of one's health

52 • The Daily Routine

page 67

This unit is vaguely based on the idea of biorhythms.

PROCEDURE: Put the students into pairs or groups. Give out the cards and ask the students to go through the questions. Bring the groups together for an all-class discussion at the end if appropriate.

TIME: 10-20 minutes

THINGS TO LOOK OUT FOR: There is lots of opportunity here to practice the simple present and the conditional.

POTENTIALLY DIFFICULT WORDS AND EXPRESSIONS: to get up, productive, to be at one's best

53 • Housework

page 68

The song **Housework** *by the B-52's would be a very cool way to introduce this activity.*

PROCEDURE: Procedure: Put the students into groups of two, three, or four, ideally with a gender mix. Give out the questionnaire, one per student, and ask the students to fill in the statements. They check the box on the left-hand side if they do the jobs, and then check the relevant boxes on the right-hand side. They should then compare and discuss.

Bring the students together for an all-class discussion at the end; allow the students to ask you your opinion.

TIME: From 10 to 20 minutes

THINGS TO LOOK OUT FOR: Teach that "like" and "hate" are usually followed by the gerund when a verb is required, e.g., "I hate ironing."

Some males are astounded at the idea that men should do housework. Personally, I think it is rather good for them to be exposed to this concept.

POTENTIALLY DIFFICULT WORDS AND EXPRESSIONS: don't mind + gerund, ironing, loading the dishwasher/washing machine, household items, trash/rubbish, chores/jobs, yard/garden (US/British difference between these pairs), communal areas, to repair

54 • Beauty

page 69

I got the idea for this unit from my friend and colleague Rebecca Llewellyn.

You could begin this activity by playing the song **You Are So Beautiful,** *a fabulous version of which was recorded by Joe Cocker. An alternative would be* **You're Beautiful** *by James Blunt.*

PROCEDURE: Put the students into groups of two, three, or four, ideally with a gender mix.
Give out the cards and ask the students to go through the questions.

Bring the students together for an all-class discussion at the end; allow the students to ask you your opinion.

TIME: From 10 to 20 minutes

THINGS TO LOOK OUT FOR: A mix of students (gender, country of origin, etc.) works well for this activity. However, it can also work with a homogenous group.

POTENTIALLY DIFFICULT WORDS AND EXPRESSIONS: reasons, makeup, plastic surgery, anti-aging creams, body lotions, beauty treatments, piercings, tattoos

55 • Sleep  *page 70*

You could introduce this topic by playing the Beatles' song 'Golden Slumbers'.

PROCEDURE: Ask the students to answer the questions alone first. Then put them into groups to discuss their answers. You can do a whole class round up afterward.

TIME: 15-25 minutes

POTENTIALLY DIFFICULT WORDS: Insomnia, sleeping tablets, enough, nightmares, productive

56 • Privacy  *page 71*

Younger learners may not respond well to this unit, although discussions about parents invading teens' privacy could be discussed. You might want to assign this for an overnight research assignment. There is a great deal of information on the Internet on this topic.

You could begin this activity by playing the song **Every Breath You Take** *by Sting and The Police and/or* **Somebody's Watching Me** *by Rockwell.*

PROCEDURE: Introduce the unit with the questions at the top of the handout. The answer to the "Big Brother" question is that it is from the novel *1984* by George Orwell, originally published at the end of the 1940s. Big Brother signifies the total control of individual freedom by the state.

Have the students work in small groups to discuss the questions. After your established time limit, the groups can report to each other, especially on questions 4 and 5.

TIME: 20 minutes, or more if you think this might be a hot topic for your students

THINGS TO LOOK FOR: Students from many countries are required to have national ID cards. Their views can be especially useful to the discussion.

POTENTIALLY DIFFICULT WORDS: privacy, invasion

57 • Alone on an Island  *page 72*

This unit was partly inspired by the long running BBC radio program '**Desert Island Discs**'.
The title track from David Gilmour's album '**On An Island**' *would a nice was to introduce this topic.*

PROCEDURE: Let the students read the description and give them around 10 minutes to think of their answers and make notes. It is OK if they don't complete each question fully. Then put them into groups and let them discuss their answers.

TIME: 20-30 minutes

THINGS TO LOOK OUT FOR: The students need to be familiar with the second conditional (If I had ..../I would take....) so it is a good idea to review this before doing this unit.

58 • Immigration  *page 73*

You could begin this activity by playing the song **Immigration Man** *by David Crosby and Graham Nash.*

PROCEDURE: Put the students into pairs. Give out the questionnaire, one per student, and ask the students to go through the questions, comparing and discussing their answers.

TIME: 10-20 minutes

THINGS TO LOOK OUT FOR: A very controversial topic, so make sure the students can handle it.

POTENTIALLY DIFFICULT WORDS AND EXPRESSIONS: to ensure economic growth, ghettos

59 • Conspiracy Theories  *page 74*

You might want to assign this for an overnight research assignment. The Internet has lots of information on these theories.

PROCEDURE: Work with the whole class to gather their answers to the questions in Part 1. The accepted answers are:

John F. Kennedy – Lee Harvey Oswald
Martin Luther King, Jr. – James Earl Ray
First man on the moon – Neil Armstrong

September 11 attacks – Al Qaeda and Osama bin Laden
Princess Diana – died accidentally in a car crash
UFOs – impossible?

Part 2. It might be best to limit the discussion to only one theory, decided upon by class vote. You could also have small groups each discuss a different theory, and then compare notes in a large group.

TIME: 10-15 minutes per theory

POTENTIALLY DIFFICULT WORDS AND EXPRESSIONS: conspiracy, theory, assassinate, right-wing

60 • America Today *page 75*

You could begin by playing the American national anthem and/or reading the words. There are also plenty of songs about America you could play as a lead-in, for example "This Land is Your Land" by Woody Guthrie, "Born in the USA" by Bruce Springsteen, "Living in America" by James Brown, or indeed many others.

You could also begin by asking the students which country was the world's superpower before America (for example, up until the Second World War, the answer would be Great Britain, which might be a surprise for younger students). Then you could ask the students to try to explain how America became the world's number-one superpower. They could even brainstorm this in groups. This can be quite interesting.

PROCEDURE: After introducing the topic, prepare the students to work in a debate format, ideally two antis debating two pros. Then give the antis the left side of the handout only, and the pros, the right side. Tell them to spend about five minutes on each statement, with an anti opening the debate using the anti statement as an opening line, and then a pro responds. Then back to the second anti and pro, continuing the debate.

TIME: 50 minutes

THINGS TO LOOK OUT FOR: It might be best to let the students choose which side they want to be on, but you may have to ask a student to argue on a side they don't like.

POTENTIALLY DIFFICULT WORDS: involve, effect, solve, superior, worship, exploit

Other Books from Pro Lingua

Conversation Strategies. 29 structured pair activities for developing strategic conversation skills at the intermediate level. Students learn the words, phrases, and conventions used by native speakers in the active give-and-take of everyday conversation.

Discussion Strategies. Carefully structured pair and small group work at the advanced-intermediate level. Excellent preparation for students who will participate in academic or professional work that requires effective participation in discussions and seminars.

Conversation Inspirations. A photocopyable collection of over 2400 conversation topics. A quick and easy source of topics to get your students talking about human nature, interpersonal relationships, and North American society. There are eight different types of activities: talks, interviews, role plays, chain stories, discussions, and three group creativity activities.

Ask and Task. A photocopyable collection of 1400 communication prompts. There are 40 topics from Advertising to Weather/Climate and Work. For each topic there are two to four pages of discussion questions and one page of tasks (activities and projects).

Surveys for Conversation. High beginner and up. You assign a questionnaire for homework. The students answer the questions on the survey and come back to class prepared to say something on the topic. Topics include family, computers, love, health, the environment, crime, clothes, shopping, and 56 others.

Improvisations. Photocopyable. High beginner to advanced. The two-page lesson format is in three parts. <u>Getting Ideas</u>: The students explore the theme through brainstorming, free writing, graphic organizers, and other activities. <u>The Story</u>: The students read a short scene that leaves much to the imagination. Finally, <u>The Improvisation</u>: The students work in groups to develop the characters and the story line, and then perform it without a script.

Thinking Deeper Photocopyable. Intermediate to advanced. 53 critical thinking/ discussion activities on important contemporary issues, problems, and solutions. Learners consider the full-color photograph, read ten or more opinion statements, record their opinions on a scale, and then explore them in a group discussion.

www.ProLinguaLearning.com

Manufactured by Amazon.ca
Bolton, ON

40033947R00061